Creating the Visitor-Centered Museum

D1475018

What does the transformation to a visitor-centered approach do for a museum? How are museums made relevant to a broad range of visitors of varying ages, identities, and social classes? Does appealing to a larger audience force museums to "dumb down" their work? What internal changes are required? Based on a multi-year, Kress Foundation–sponsored study of ten innovative American and European collections-based museums recognized by their peers to be visitor centered, Peter Samis and Mimi Michaelson answer these key questions for the field. The book

- describes key institutions that have opened the doors to a wider range of visitors;
- addresses the internal struggles to reorganize and democratize these institutions;
- uses case studies, interviews of key personnel, Key Takeaways, and additional resources to help museum professionals implement a visitor-centered approach in collections-based institutions.

Peter Samis is Associate Curator of Interpretation at the San Francisco Museum of Modern Art, USA. He previously spearheaded the museum's award-winning Interactive Educational Technology programs for many years and also served as an Adjunct Professor on the Technology-Enhanced Communication for Cultural Heritage (TEC-CH) program at the University of Lugano, Switzerland.

Mimi Michaelson is an education and museum consultant. She received her doctorate in Human Development and Psychology from Harvard University, USA, where she also managed Project Zero's Good Work project for many years.

Creating the Visitor-Centered Museum

Peter Samis and Mimi Michaelson

Only connect!
Peter S. Samis

Routledge
Taylor & Francis Group

NEW YORK AND LONDON

First published 2017
by Routledge
711 Third Avenue, New York, NY 10017

and by Routledge
2 Park Square, Milton Park, Abingdon, Oxon OX14 4RN

Routledge is an imprint of the Taylor & Francis Group, an informa business

British Library Cataloguing in Publication Data
A catalogue record for this book is available from the British Library

Library of Congress Cataloging-in-Publication Data
Names: Samis, Peter S., author. | Michaelson, Mimi, author.
Title: Creating the visitor-centered museum / Peter Samis and
    Mimi Michaelson.
Description: First edition. | New York, NY : Routledge, [2016] |
    Includes bibliographical references.
Identifiers: LCCN 2016007452 | ISBN 9781138693265 (hardback :
    alk. paper) | ISBN 9781138693272 (pbk. : alk. paper) |
    ISBN 9781315531014 (ebook) Subjects: LCSH: Museums—
    Management. | Museums—Management—Case studies. |
    Museum visitors. Curatorial studies.
Classification: LCC AM121 .S35 2016 | DDC 069.068—dc23
LC record available at http://lccn.loc.gov/2016007452

ISBN: 978-1-629-58190-3 (hbk)
ISBN: 978-1-629-58191-0 (pbk)
ISBN: 978-1-315-53101-4 (ebk)

Cover design by James Brendan Williams
Typeset in Sabon
by Apex CoVantage, LLC

"Objecthood doesn't have a place in the world if there's not an individual person making use of that object."

—Olafur Eliasson

"Only connect—"

—E. M. Forster, epigraph to *Howard's End*

Contents

List of Figures   ix
List of Tables   xii
Figure Acknowledgments   xiii
Acknowledgments   xiv

PART ONE
Introduction: Setting the Stage   1

 1 Considering the Visitor   9

 2 Change Takes Leadership: Moments of Personal
    Transformation   20

 3 Contours of Change   27

PART TWO
Case Studies   45

I   Charting History   47

 4 Denver Art Museum: Building a Sustainable
    Visitor-Centered Practice   49

II Engaging through Audience Immersion   63

 5 City Museum: The Power of Play   65

 6 Ruhr Museum: Connecting through Adaptive Reuse
    and Design   70

 7 Minnesota History Center: Lessons from a Learning Team   82

III Reinvigorating Traditional Museums   91

  8 Detroit Institute of Arts: Reinventing a Landmark Museum
     with and for Visitors   93

  9 Oakland Museum of California: Including a
     Diverse Public   105

10 Columbus Museum of Art: Museum as Community
     Living Room   114

IV Creating Social Change   127

11 Kelvingrove: Museum as Cultural Commons   129

V Taking a Critical Stance on Museum Practice   143

12 Van Abbe Museum: Radicality Meets Hospitality   145

13 Museum of Contemporary Art Denver: Experience
     over Objects   155

PART THREE
Conclusion: Varieties of Visitor-Centeredness and Change   163

14 Conclusion: Varieties of Visitor-Centeredness
     and Organizational Change   165

Appendix A: Method   177
Appendix B: Adult Gallery Activities at
    the Denver Art Museum   179
Appendix C: Make-Up of DIA Visitor Panels   180
Bibliography   181
Index   188

Figures

1.1   Ice skates exhibited at Canadian Museum of Civilization.   11
1.2   Olafur Eliasson's *The Weather Project* in the Turbine Hall
      at Tate Modern.   12
1.3   Anish Kapoor's *Cloud Gate* in Chicago's Millennium Park.   13
3.1   The Change Cycle.   33
4.1   Denver Art Museum: seating in the Asian Art galleries.   50
4.2a–b   Denver Art Museum: Two views of the Discovery
      Library.   53
4.3a–b   Denver Art Museum: Laminated "human connection
      cards" in the galleries.   55
4.4   Denver Art Museum Contemporary Galleries: facing a portrait
      wall, comfortable seating and a coffee table on which a creative
      challenge is placed: "Write a biography in six words."   56
4.5   Denver Art Museum: treasure hunt Bingo cards placed
      at child height.   57
4.6   Denver Art Museum: visitors in a maker space adjacent
      to the galleries.   58
5.1   City Museum: children in aerial tubes above "Monster"
      playground.   66
5.2   City Museum: first floor grotto, reached via a ten-story
      slide.   66
6.1   Ruhr Museum: exterior view.   71
6.2   Ruhr Museum: ascending the seven-story ribbon
      of escalator.   72
6.3   Ruhr Museum: descending into the exhibits guided
      by a tablet.   73
6.4   Ruhr Museum: *The Present: Signs of the Times*. Entrance.   75
6.5   Ruhr Museum: *Signs of the Times*. First object in exhibit.   76
6.6   Ruhr Museum: *Signs of the Times*. Exhibit of doll furniture.   77
6.7   Ruhr Museum: *Signs of the Times*. Exhibit of beer bottles
      with Chinese labels.   77
6.8   Ruhr Museum: 12-Meter Level (History).   78

6.9 Ruhr Museum: parade of native species on the
      12-Meter Level.   79
6.10 Ruhr Museum: artifact and information "conveyors"
      at 6-Meter Level.   80
7.1 Minnesota History Center: *Open House.* A domestic
      interior with original stories, not original artifacts.   85
7.2 *Minnesota's Greatest Generation:* set portraying a
      dry cleaning shop, displaying uniforms and garments
      worn in the 1960s.   86
7.3 Minnesota History Center: exhibition prototyping.   88
7.4 Minnesota History Center: two comments left by
      Dakota Indians.   89
8.1 Detroit Institute of Arts: *Splendor by the Hour* in the
      European decorative arts galleries.   94
8.2 Detroit Institute of Arts: *Splendor by the Hour*
      video banquet.   95
8.3 Detroit Institute of Arts: "pull-out panel." The darker
      ovals each connect to a short commentary.   100
8.4a–c Detroit Institute of Arts: Richard Long's sculpture
      Stone Line with "layered label."   101
9.1 Oakland Museum of California: "Cultures Meet"
      in OMCA's History galleries.   107
9.2 Oakland Museum of California: *You Are Here* in
      the California Portrait Gallery.   111
10.1 Columbus Museum of Art: Impressionist landscapes
      with visible voting poll.   119
10.2a–e Columbus Museum of Art: five frames from the
      MUSEUM DOs & DON'Ts video.   123
10.3 Columbus Museum of Art: child-friendly display
      demonstrates reason for "No Touching" policy.   124
10.4a–d Columbus Museum of Art: Wonder Room.   124
10.5 Columbus Museum of Art: an intimate moment in the
      "Love and War" gallery.   125
11.1 Kelvingrove Art Gallery and Museum in Kelvingrove
      Park, Glasgow.   130
11.2 Kelvingrove: articulated armor meets its armadillo
      inspiration in *Conflict and Consequence* gallery.   131
11.3a–b Kelvingrove: painting and object label. Note brevity
      of text and reversal of standard label hierarchy.   134
11.4 Kelvingrove: Raoul Dufy painting with story-based
      touchscreen interactive, both at child height.   135
11.5a–b Kelvingrove: touchscreen kiosk below John Pettie
      painting leads visitors through the heroine's suitor
      selection, with the terms of her choices updated to reflect
      contemporary Glasgow life.   136

11.6a–b   Glasgow Museums Resource Centre, Nitshill: open
storage with painting racks arranged by theme; early
communications technology.   139
11.6c–d   Glasgow Museums Resource Centre: open storage with
1910 butcher's van; Rolls-Royce test engine for the
Concorde supersonic plane.   140
11.7   Glasgow Museums Resource Centre: school kids on field trip.   140
12.1   Van Abbe Museum: 3-D sculpture made in 2009 after
El Lissitzky's *New Man*, 1923 (as interpreted by
Prof. John Milner and produced by Henry Milner, 2009).   148
12.2   Van Abbe Museum: El Lissitzky galleries with display
cases for ephemera on left and computer-based slide
show inset in wall.   148
12.3a–b   Van Abbe Museum: El Lissitzky quote with Nedko
Solakov commentary.   149
12.4   Van Abbe Museum: another Lissitzky quote with
Solakov repartee: "A GOD is playing with/a constructivist
puzzle/desperately trying to create a black Square."   149
12.5a–b   Van Abbe Museum: object labels with space above
for tags contributed by curators and visitors.   150
12.6   Van Abbe Museum: Game Master with visitor using
the Journey Recorder table in *Play Van Abbe 4:
The Pilgrim, the Tourist, the Flaneur (and the Worker)*.   152

Tables

0.1   Museums Studied   3
P2.1 Six Elements Common to Visitor-Centered Museums   45
P2.2 An Approach to Organizing the Museums Treated
      in This Book   46
14.1 Continuum of Approaches to Connecting with Visitors   165

Figure Acknowledgments

Acknowledgments

This book grew out of a shared question about what engages visitors in museums, raised many years ago when Peter and Mimi first met and spent hours debating this topic in the SFMOMA galleries. Since then, the ideas have evolved and we have enjoyed the support of many in the development of our thinking.

With a dare on the Washington, DC, Metro, Kris Wetterlund further sparked the book's growth; she and Christina Olsen then both introduced us to Max Marmor and the Kress Foundation as potential sponsors of research on "best practices in museum interpretation." Zahava Doering gave us hospitality and both she and Nancy Proctor gave us encouragement as we incubated our ideas and turned them into a proposal.

Inevitably, the topic transmuted as our research began: on the one hand, we came to understand that there was no one set of "best practices," but rather solutions best suited for particular audiences and situations. Secondly, our interviews with practitioners at museums nominated as sites of interpretive excellence revealed their consistent efforts to overcome an entrenched dynamic that ran through the field: the division between "curatorial scholarship" and "community relevance." Each institution we visited was committed to finding ways to bridge this gap, often reconfiguring staff and processes to turn that tension into a creative spark.

Our next set of thank yous goes to those museum practitioners—directors, curators, experience designers, project managers, evaluators, interpretive specialists, and many more—who sat with us and generously shared their goals and frustrations, war stories and success stories, internal processes, and pragmatic solutions. Everywhere we went we were amazed by how passionately these colleagues cared about what they did every day, and how committed they were to turning their institutions' mission statements into a tangible reality. A full list of those we interviewed is in Appendix A, but we take this opportunity to single out the museum directors:

Graham W. J. Beal, Detroit Institute of Arts
Ulrich Borsdorf, Ruhr Museum
Rick Erwin III, City Museum, St. Louis

Charles Esche, Van Abbe Museum
Lori Fogarty, Oakland Museum of California
Christoph Heinrich, Denver Art Museum
Adam Lerner, Museum of Contemporary Art, Denver
Nannette Maciejunes, Columbus Museum of Art
Mark O'Neill, Glasgow Life (former Director of Kelvingrove)
Dan Spock, Minnesota History Center

These directors welcomed us, even at the risk of exposing sometimes con-flictual internal processes, the better to advance visitor-centered practice in the field as a whole.

Readers of an earlier version of this manuscript gave us crucial insights that led to its reshaping: our thanks go to Deena Chalabi, Randi Korn, Dana Mitroff Silvers, and Susan Rome. Many others served, wittingly or un-, as discussants on specific points.

For immeasurably improving our manuscript, we are also indebted to Carla Sinz, who deftly wielded her editor's pen.

Of course, none of this would have happened without the support of the Samuel H. Kress Foundation, which underwrote Mimi's work on the project as well as the research and interviews that form the heart of this book. A Kress Summer Fellowship in Museum Education at the Sterling and Fran-cine Clark Art Institute enabled us to come together from our bi-coastal locations in a bucolic New England setting to hash out lessons learned and the chapter structure. Finally, a Kress subsidy is allowing Routledge to print this book in color. Our thanks to Max Marmor, Wyman Meers, Lisa Schermerhorn, the Kress Foundation Board and staff are deep; we only hope the product proves a worthy contribution to the field and repays their trust.

Our hosts and colleagues in the Visiting Scholars program at The Clark added another essential dimension to this book's formative journey, includ-ing in-depth seminar discussions with scholar-curators about how museums might live up to their full public mandate. In Europe, Dr. Harald Kraemer shared his vision at museum sites that emphasized the primacy of perception.

We owe a debt of thanks to our fiscal sponsors: the San Francisco Museum of Modern Art and Museum-Ed. SFMOMA has been consistently support-ive of Peter's involvement in this project, giving him work-related leave for research, writing, and the Clark residency. Special thanks go to Neal Bene-zra, Ruth Berson, and Chad Coerver. Museum-Ed picked up the torch and helped us carry this manuscript to publication. This book could not have happened without the ongoing support of both entities.

Speaking of support close to home, on a more personal level, each of us owes a great debt to our spouses: Peter's life partner Mary Curtis Ratcliff and Mimi's husband Brian Dowley. They have truly been our coaches: patient, steadfast, encouraging us to stay the course to reach our goal. They could well be called the champions of this sometimes challenging, jointly authored manuscript.

On a personal note, Peter wishes to thank his 92-year-old mother, still alive, who taught him the love of art, and his father, now deceased, who inculcated the ethos of community service. Speaking of community, he sends a shout-out to the *barristas* of Berkeley, witnesses to his many weekend and late-night writing sessions!

Mimi remains grateful for the foundational teachings offered by early mentors: Howard Gardner, Mihalyi Csikszentmihalyi, and Bill Damon; as well as for the lessons gleaned about the arts, research and thinking from Shari Tishman and other colleagues at Project Zero. Mimi also sends a nod to Michael, Charlie, Luke, and Malcolm, as they continue to remind her of the importance of youthful perspectives.

This book wouldn't have happened without Mitch Allen of Left Coast Press, our originating editor. His sage counsel and conviction that the book had an important place in the museum literature kept us going through all the iterations of the manuscript. Ryan Harris did the early production work, preparing text and images for Routledge. At Routledge, we have worked with Elizabeth Thomasson and Anna Callander, and Katherine Wetzel of Apex CoVantage has managed the production process. Our thanks to all involved!

Now that the book is done, its life truly begins. We hereby acknowledge you, our readers, fellow practitioners, and your dedication to making our museums worthy sites of community meaning-making, experience, and exchange.

Note: Graham Beal and Ulrich Borsdorf have retired since the interviews conducted for this book.

Part One

Introduction

Setting the Stage

Replete with their own histories and missions, museums come with varied stories and metaphors. From treasure chest to learning lab, museums mean different things to different people. This is not a new story, nor a stagnant one. In fact, diversity of purpose and institutional change go hand in hand as natural parts of cultural evolution, leading to innovation in the field. It is not surprising that museums around the world are again changing, this time with many in transition toward a more visitor-centered future. What this visitor-centered change looks like and what the players reveal about the process provides the substance of our story. In the pages that follow we share a glimpse of some of the transformations we have witnessed and the voices of those leading the way.

> I don't think museums, as they have existed and existed for a hundred years are going to survive if they don't make changes—even with billionaires on the board, even with some of the huge resources that some institutions have.[1]

These are the words of a well-respected museum director talking about the inevitability of change in today's museums. Directors, many of whom have worked in the field for decades, spoke with us about dramatic transitions currently taking place. Talking about how museums need to evolve to stay relevant, the director continues:

> I really do think that if they are going to be vital—you know, they may be able to survive financially, but will they truly be sustainable within their communities, as places that are really connected to their community? It's going to be a reality that there are going to have to be some changes.

As the director notes, many of the transitions have to do with museums reaching out to the community—to visitors and potential visitors—in new and authentic ways. While the degree may vary, in some cases the modifications are dramatic, involving a fundamental reconsideration of mission and how the museum itself is structured. Everyone connected to the museum is potentially impacted—both visitors and staff alike.

These kinds of transformations inevitably give rise to a debate that places museum directors, curators, exhibition designers, and educators at center stage in a dialogue about audience. Ultimately, the debate is focused on bringing to life the notion of a visitor-centered museum: a museum where audience matters as much as collections. As one interviewee said: "We have to keep reevaluating: Who's our audience and what do they need from us?" For a visitor-centered museum, these questions are the starting point of all museum business.

In this book we explore aspects of this ongoing debate. We begin with the premise that the debate is good, an inevitable part of a process that moves everyone forward. We don't suggest that change is easy, but do endorse the idea that the challenge is worthwhile. We also believe that the current focus—a new audience-centered paradigm—is here to stay. This new vantage point carries other essential elements with it, including the need to honor multiple voices and multiple sources of knowledge. Furthermore, to meet the variety of needs that come with a more diverse public, an array of approaches or "entry points" is vital.

We understand that the term "visitor-centered" is sometimes highly charged. On the one hand, it can represent a banner and rallying cry for educators who interact daily with visitors and see missed opportunities for connection with the public. On the other hand, that banner can turn into a red flag for curators, who fear that it may mean they need to let visitors define the messages—and even the exhibitions—they present. That is not our intent here. What we do suggest is that understanding where visitors are coming from helps us understand how to engage them in a dialogue that is meaningful to all. It allows us to connect with our audience even as we honor the expertise of museum professionals, including curators, educators, designers, et al. We use the term "visitor-centered" because we believe visitors are a population that museums have historically been happier to speak to than to listen to—and that real two-way communication is what visitors deserve.

In the pages that follow, we present examples of innovative visitor-centered practice and museums in transition. These two threads—visitor-centered interpretation and museum change—form the foundation of this book.

The Study

What does it mean for a museum of art or history to really be visitor centered? With the generous support of the Samuel H. Kress Foundation, five years ago we began a study to address this question. We visited twenty museums, studying ten of those institutions in depth: seven in the United States and three in Europe. The museums were chosen following a query sent to more than fifty colleagues in the United States and Europe soliciting nominations for examples of innovative visitor-centered practice. Colleagues were

Table 0.1 Museums Studied

In-Depth: Site Visit + Interviews	Site Visit Only
Oakland Museum of California	Tropenmuseum, Amsterdam
Detroit Institute of Arts	Amstelkring, Amsterdam
Columbus Museum of Art	Boijmans van Beuningen, Rotterdam
Ruhr Museum, Essen, Germany	Museum Insel Hombroich, Neuss, Germany
Van Abbe Museum, Eindhoven, NL	Riverside Museum, Glasgow
Kelvingrove Gallery, Glasgow, UK	Gallery of Modern Art, Glasgow
Denver Art Museum	Nitshill Open Storage Facility, Glasgow
Museum of Contemporary Art, Denver*	Walker Art Center, Minneapolis
Minnesota History Center	Minneapolis Institute of Arts
City Museum, St. Louis	The Pulitzer Foundation, St. Louis

*Site not studied in depth; select interviews conducted only.

asked to nominate museums with exemplary interpretive practices regardless of size or type, and to highlight the criteria that informed their choice. In selecting our final set to visit we prioritized art museums because historically they have been underachievers in this area, and we wanted to see what examples those art museums that have taken this path could provide. That said, we kept in mind that other types of museums have been pioneering visitor-centered approaches for years—approaches from which all museum practitioners might have much to learn.

As much as possible, we tell this story through the voices of those interviewed, making plentiful use of excerpts from the thirty-two interviews we conducted—eleven with directors, and seven each with curators, educator-interpretive specialists, and cross-departmental teams. These quotes convey a sense of the drama, the stakes, and the dedication of the colleagues engaged in implementing a visitor-centered mission.[2]

The limited time spent in each museum's galleries—one day—precluded conducting on-site visitor research ourselves. For this reason we gave preference in our selection process to museums that had already conducted extensive evaluations in their galleries. We are aware that it might seem ironic to be talking about visitor-centered museums without having taken the time to study the visitors within them, but our primary purpose here is to speak to museum professionals from the perspective of their peers. For a more detailed discussion of Methods, see Appendix A.

The Authors

This book is written from two points of view: one of the authors is a long-time museum professional; the other comes from social science research. Peter has worked in both curatorial and educational roles, and been a pioneer in the use of digital technology in museums. Over the years, Peter has observed an interesting dichotomy, particularly prevalent in art museums: on the one hand, museums are increasingly eager to embrace portable technology as a way to provide interpretive information without disrupting the visual field of the gallery; on the other, the majority of art museum visitors do not choose to use these technologies. For Peter, a primary research question that inspired this study was: *What are museums doing for these visitors?*

Mimi has a doctorate in Human Development and Psychology and studied creativity and cognitive development. As a former Project Zero manager, she has broad research experience, including as Senior Project Manager of Harvard's Good Work project. Combining interests in moral action and creativity, Mimi's concern is in how museums see their social mission and in their promise as centers of engagement.[3] For Mimi, a primary question that inspired this work was: *How do museums see their social mission as the mission extends to meaningfully engage broader audiences?*

Peter and Mimi have long held a joint interest in what kinds of interactions or experiences attract and stick over time—what we call *Visual Velcro*.[4]

Each of us brings our particular background as lens and bias to the work. We hope these different perspectives are also a strength.

Documenting Two Types of Change

We started out looking for innovative visitor-centered interpretive practices, yet we discovered something more: a visitor-centered focus leads to organizational transformation. The two are so integral to each other that we found they had to be considered in tandem. This book grew out of the exploration of these two intersecting trails. Adopting a visitor-centered approach to exhibition development often leads to structural change in the museum itself, including new museum roles and forms of staff collaboration. The latter phenomenon was discovered en route, the former by design.

A Visitor-Centered Approach in Exhibitions

By our definition, a visitor-centered approach puts collections/exhibitions and visitor experience on equal footing. The museum cares about visitor experience in the galleries and solicits visitor input in crafting these experiences. From this vantage point, visitors matter as much as collections do—ideally, for everyone who works in the museum. In the museums we visited, there is a level of buy-in from the staff. While there may not be equal enthusiasm from all, staff commitment is not incidental, but crucial. Successful directors work to increase this level of commitment.

Collection care and research continue to be important, as do the many logistical and financial aspects of running a museum, but they are integrated with a visitor-centered goal. Furthermore, these museums often demonstrate a desire to reach beyond their traditional core audiences to a much broader community. Reaching an expanded audience is deemed central to the new museum mission.

As a baseline, a visitor-centered approach requires museum staff to find ways to welcome visitors in a wide variety of ways: offering plentiful and comfortable seating, clear and interesting labels tailored to audience interests, family-focused spaces or activities, and helpful staff. (See sidebar: Judy Rand's *Visitors' Bill of Rights*.) Such museums move beyond a focus on subject expertise. Significantly, the welcome remains present in the gallery even when no live programming or tours are happening. In other words, there are welcoming and engaging components even when a visitor is *alone* in an exhibition. The museum provides entry points for a broad spectrum of people to connect on their own terms. Ultimately, the forms of engagement—analog or digital, mobile or fixed—matter less than the sensitivity to audience needs that is evidenced in their design.

Judy Rand's *Visitors' Bill of Rights*[5]

A list of important human needs, seen from the visitors' point of view:

1) Comfort: "Meet my basic needs."
   Visitors need fast, easy, obvious access to clean, safe, barrier-free restrooms, fountains, food, baby-changing tables, and plenty of seating. They also need full access to exhibits.
2) Orientation: "Make it easy for me to find my way around."
   Visitors need to make sense of their surroundings. Clear signs and well-planned spaces help them know what to expect, where to go, how to get there, and what it's about.
3) Welcome/belonging: "Make me feel welcome."
   Friendly staff make visitors feel more at ease. If visitors see themselves represented in exhibits and programs and on the staff, they'll feel more like they belong.
4) Enjoyment: "I want to have fun."
   Visitors want to have a good time. If they run into barriers (like broken exhibits, activities they can't relate to, intimidating labels) they can feel frustrated, bored, or confused.
5) Socializing: "I came to spend time with my family and friends."
   Visitors come for a social outing with family and friends (or to connect with society at large). They expect to talk, interact, and share the experience; exhibits can set the stage for this.
6) Respect: "Accept me for who I am and what I know."
   Visitors want to be accepted at their own level of knowledge and interest. They don't want exhibits, labels, or staff to exclude them, patronize them, or make them feel dumb.

7) Communication: "Help me understand and let me talk, too."
   Visitors need accuracy, honesty, and clear communication from labels, programs, staff, and volunteers. They want to ask questions and express differing points of view.

8) Learning: "I want to learn something new."
   Visitors come (and bring the kids) "to learn something new," but they learn it different ways. It's important to know how visitors learn, and assess their knowledge and interests. Controlling distractions (like crowds, noise, and information overload) helps them too.

9) Choice and control: "Let me choose; give me some control."
   Visitors need some autonomy: freedom to choose, and exert some control, touching and getting close to whatever they can. They need to use their bodies and move around freely.

10) Challenge and confidence: "Give me a challenge I know I can handle."
    Visitors want to succeed. A task that's too easy bores them; too hard makes them anxious. Providing a wide variety of experiences will match their wide range of skills.

11) Revitalization: "Help me leave refreshed, restored."
    When visitors are focused, fully engaged, and enjoying themselves, time flies and they feel refreshed: a "flow" experience that exhibits can aim to create.

Structural Change

When we speak of structural change, we refer to a reconsideration of key museum roles by the museum leadership itself—for example, revisiting the role or tasks associated with curators, educators, or designers and the relations between them. Revisited roles entail changes in how professionals work together, including the tasks people take on and the make-up of collaborative teams. These changes often impact who leads a team or takes final responsibility for an end product. Most museums have long-established and clearly defined protocols and hierarchies. New ways of working ultimately shift traditional structures and may end up equalizing roles or flattening hierarchies.

Stemming from their training, each group knows its territory and its discipline, often working on its own in its well-understood domain. While each of the traditional roles continues to be important, as visitors' needs become more central we witness a questioning and changing of the boundaries between traditional positions—in particular among those most directly tied to exhibition development: curators, educators, and exhibition designers. Not surprisingly, these are the areas where we also saw the most organizational tension.

A consequence of each group working within its own territory is that roles have traditionally been highly segmented, and departments siloed. However, in our interviews, along with the shifting of traditional roles we also heard a shaking of the silo mentality. We saw new teams, with new members, leaders, and duties—and most importantly, a new outlook. Of course, accompanying this change, new challenges surface.

Taken together, the movement toward a visitor-centered approach and shifting museum roles and structures are combining to transform the museum world. In fact, while these changes are not universal, and may even be slow in coming, we believe that their impact will redefine how museums operate in the years to come.

Notes

1 To protect subjects, we selectively protect the anonymity of the speakers.
2 When not specified otherwise, the voices woven throughout the narrative come from these interviews.
3 Understood as related to "*vital engagement,* an absorbing and meaningful relationship between self and world," J. Nakamura (2001).
4 Peter Samis. "New Technologies as Part of a Comprehensive Interpretive Plan." In Phyllis Hecht and Herminia Din (Eds.), *The Digital Museum: A Think Guide.* Washington, DC: American Association of Museums, 2007, pp. 19–34.
5 Judy Rand. Reprinted by permission of the author.

1 Considering the Visitor

The Intimidating Museum

We could be walking into a church—the entry flanked by oversized Doric columns and the drama that comes with vaulted ceilings. We may even see stained glass windows, although no altar. We venture in, past the stoic guards that mimic statues. And immediately, we see objects. They are important, precious, encased behind glass with a lengthy narrative attached. Not knowing anything about these objects or the painting on the wall above, we already feel overwhelmed and out of place. Our voices echo back and we are inclined to whisper in this hallowed cultural shrine.

Museums enjoy tremendous prestige in contemporary culture. Our institutions are trusted arbiters of taste and quality. Visitors and non-visitors defer to museum expertise, even if they don't like what they see within our walls, or come to see it very often. One reason they may not visit is that, whether they admit it or not, many people are downright befuddled by the objects in our galleries. Decidedly, museums can be baffling, bewildering places, where even the physical space can be intimidating. With limited knowledge or context, even easy works—the pleasing or seemingly recognizable ones—may be hard to understand.

As a distinguished curator admits, "Contemporary art remains deeply enigmatic and obscure to most people." While being faced with obscure works may be a common concern for art museums, other types of museums also share the challenge of making objects more meaningful. It's hardly too bold to say that the first priority of museums has not always been to make visitors feel welcome—or objects less difficult to understand. Small wonder that the general public approaches museums with temerity. Meanwhile, those working in museums are equally ambivalent about how far they want to go to make visitors feel at home.

One museum director told us how surprised she was when a group of museum trustees was at a loss while looking at art in their own museum.

After greeting the group in the museum lobby, the director was called away to the phone:

> I said, "I'm sorry, I have to take this call. Why don't you all just, you know, go upstairs, look around. You know, just enjoy the museum and I'll be right back, in ten or fifteen minutes."
>
> I came back out and they were all still standing in the lobby. And I said, "Why are we all in the lobby, still?" And they said, "Well, we didn't really know what to do when you're not there, so we just stayed here." I was shocked. To realize that people that close to the institution would even own up to the fact that they weren't exactly sure what they were supposed to do in the galleries was shocking to me, as someone who had come out of a curatorial background. . . . I, like all curators, sort of assumed that people understood, and didn't realize that we were all talking in this sort of hermetic language that spoke to other art people, but not necessarily to a broader community of people.

As the director, a former curator herself, notes, she was blind to her own assumptions about visitors' comfort in the museum. She was shocked to learn that museum trustees were so intimidated by the museum that without a guide they preferred to simply remain in the lobby. In myriad ways the plight of these trustees, unsure of appropriate museum behavior or insecure in their own knowledge, is exacerbated among the broader public. This story vividly illustrates the challenge: Museums are intimidating spaces with a language all their own. Even trustees get stalled in the entry. As long as the museum is providing interpretive assistance, visitors can feel supported. But most museum visitors don't have the luxury of a director, curator, or a docent to guide them. What then, are we giving visitors who try to make sense of these unfamiliar surroundings on their own?

Offering Interpretive Hooks

Some artworks or objects don't need much supplementary framing to captivate people. We say these objects have *Visual Velcro*. These are the charismatic or iconic objects—the ones that always draw a crowd. Anything with a face on it or a famous name attached stands a better chance. Well-known cultural artifacts such as the *Spirit of St. Louis* come complete with a story that bears retelling. Other works or objects seem like they were made from a different mid-century miracle material: Teflon. Much of the Minimalist art of the 1960s, for instance, still leaves uninitiated viewers baffled. Their gaze just slips right off one piece and on to the next . . . and shortly thereafter, out of the gallery. But once a visitor has some hooks, or scaffolding, the very pieces that seemed to merit scant attention can become fascinating sensory and cognitive explorations.

The work of interpretation, then, is to give hooks to the hookless, and ensure that these hooks are sufficiently varied that they can successfully land in the mental fabric of a broad array of visitors.[1] Of course, this is where understanding of audience is critical: there are many different kinds of audiences and what is needed is an equally broad array of hooks. Once visitors have a framework, all kinds of impressions, emotions, and reflections can weave themselves into the fabric of cognition, or experience. This is true for all kinds of objects—not simply challenging pieces of contemporary art. Here's an example:

Figure 1.1 Ice skates exhibited at Canadian Museum of Civilization. Courtesy
    SkateNY.com.

While most people can name the objects above, few are particularly impressed by them. It is only when we are told that these are the skates worn by the famous Canadian hockey player Wayne Gretzky, "The Great One," as a child that the picture snaps into focus. *Now we get it.* Visitors to museums are constantly looking for the inside information that will help *them* get it too.

   Do we overestimate the ability of objects to speak for themselves? Are we prepared to put them to the test? The problem with this, of course, is that when we speak of putting our objects to the test, it ends up being the visitors who feel tested. And no one likes to be tested and come up wanting. Most objects have limited communicative power and visitors need our help in understanding their importance. Counting on respect, visitors end up relying on the largesse of museums to share their knowledge. When we don't welcome visitors—or meet them halfway—we run the risk of pushing them away.

This lack of context is one of the greatest challenges facing modern and contemporary art museums in particular. The very environment we treat as the baseline for art experience—the white cube gallery space—can be off-putting and alienating to visitors. "Why are the walls so white?" asked one group of teenagers polled by a subject museum. "It feels like a hospital in here."

Of course, museum white is the color tone that reads to the art world as a universal background; it instantly renders any object placed in front of it, be it a painting or an assemblage of scrap metal, legible as art. However, for others, it strips away all context and meaning, and leaves them without a clue as to how to approach the work.

Figure 1.2 Olafur Eliasson's *The Weather Project* in the Turbine Hall at Tate Modern. Viewers lying on the floor saw themselves reflected in the mirrored ceiling above.

At the opposite end of the spectrum are works and environments that are themselves immersive, and have proven engaging to a broad public: Jeff Koons' four-story flowering *Puppy* outside the Guggenheim Bilbao; Carsten Höller's giant sliding ponds at Tate and New York's New Museum; Olafur Eliasson's *The Weather Project* at Tate, which turned a huge concrete slab floor into a virtual beach for sun-starved Londoners in the winter of 2003; and many more. Over the past decade or more, immersive artworks have increasingly dominated both art biennials (which cater to crowds of art aficionados) and public sculpture (which caters to less trained crowds of visitors). We see this at Chicago's Millennium Park, which combines a sculptural bandshell by architect Frank Gehry with Anish Kapoor's *Cloud Gate* and Jaume Plensa's *Crown Fountain*.

While critics might balk at these "spectacles," the artworks do have the virtue of bearing their context with them: for example, through its curving, continuously mirrored surface, *Cloud Gate* transforms the Chicago skyline around it, the people who walk under it, and the sky above into the ultimate "selfie." It acts as an optical device that generates a constantly changing mirror image of its viewers with friends, strangers, or the built environment. That intense and effortless experience of situatedness might not carry with it the prestige of "difficult art," but it leaves an indelible impression on those who experience it. It reaches out and attaches, like Velcro.

What do we do with more cerebral, less charismatic or sensational works? Works that fail to carry their context with them? In those situations, it is

Figure. 1.3 Anish Kapoor's *Cloud Gate* in Chicago's Millennium Park.

incumbent upon us as museum practitioners to go the extra mile ourselves, to demonstrate a double empathy: toward both the artist or object and toward the novice viewer. We need worry less about connoisseurs; they tend to take care of themselves. They bring their context and finely tuned perceptual skills with them. On the other hand, whether with abstract or conceptual art, art from other traditions and sometimes even with ice skates, novice viewers do not know where to begin.[2]

Freeman Tilden's Six Principles of Interpretive Communication[3]

Freeman Tilden (1883–1980), a pioneering figure in the US National Parks Service, formulated the following guidelines for thinking about—and developing—interpretation. They are just as applicable to history and art museums as they are to nature and wildlife.

1. Any interpretation that does not somehow relate what is being displayed or described to something within the personality or experience of the visitor will be sterile.
2. Information, as such, is not Interpretation. Interpretation is revelation based on information. But they are entirely different things. However, all interpretation includes information.
3. Interpretation is an art, which combines many arts, whether the materials presented are scientific, historical, or architectural. Any art is to some degree teachable.
4. The chief aim of Interpretation is not instruction, but provocation.
5. Interpretation should aim to present a whole rather than a part, and must address itself to the whole person rather than any phase.
6. Interpretation addressed to children (say, up to the age of twelve) should not be a dilution of the presentation to adults, but should follow a fundamentally different approach. To be at its best it will require a separate program.

History Repeats

Growing out of earlier visitor research, the current debate about the importance of listening to visitors is hardly new. In fact, a Getty-funded study titled *Insights: Museums, Visitors, Attitudes, and Expectations: A Focus Group Experiment*, documents a series of focus groups that began at the Art Institute of Chicago way back in 1987. The following year the research continued at ten other museums from coast to coast, culminating in a symposium held at The Getty in 1989.

The simple goal of that research was "to learn more about the museum as visitors actually experienced it" and "to stimulate interdisciplinary communications and problem-solving within the museum." In other words, to gather first-hand information about what visitors were looking for and stimulate a dialogue among museum professionals.

At each institution, three kinds of focus groups were held: those with cross-departmental staff members, those with visitors, and those with non-visitors. In the case of the last two (visitors and non-visitors), three sessions each were conducted: the first to elicit expectations about their upcoming museum visit, the second consisting of the visit itself, with visitors' impressions recorded through an annotated diary, and the third to debrief the participants about their museum experience. Alan Newman, the facilitator who conducted the groups, summarized the findings:

> Both first-time and repeat visitors told us they wanted information—more information—so they can learn about what they are seeing. They told us when more information was provided, their appreciation of the objects increased. It seems that the more visitors are told about an object and its background, the greater the likelihood of their connection to it.[4]

The formula is not complex: information leads to greater understanding and appreciation. As far back as 1989 visitors were asking for more information, looking to the museum to provide lost context. Velcro. A story to hold onto, to situate the significance of an object. And what types of information did they want? Predictably, the information requested then was similar to what people still request today: an art context, information about the artist's life, the object's historic significance, the background of the culture or period, and information about the artist's technique.[5] In effect, what the visitors wanted most of all was "to know what makes it an important work of art."

The Getty study reminds us that without training in art history—or for that matter, history, natural history, or science—museum visitors need help in understanding the story behind an object and why it is on display. While the research focused on art museums, the findings could easily apply more broadly to include other types of museums as well. Without information or context, visitors only get so far in making sense of an object's relevance—not to mention why it's deemed important enough to win a permanent place in a museum.

The Getty report continued: "In short, visitors told us that they want information that promotes learning and reduces intimidation." To emphasize that these were not isolated opinions, Newman notes that these findings were consistent across all eleven museums. One could say they were endemic in the way museums did business. They were structural.[6]

At the same conference, the influential social psychologist Mihalyi Csik-szentmihalyi interpreted the focus group findings this way:

> Total immersion in the work of art is the magic experts and layper-sons alike hope for when they visit a museum, but rarely attain . . . Yet most potential museum visitors just do not know what they are supposed to do in front of a work of art. [They] are very aware that they sorely lack the background for getting the full benefit of what they are exposed to.[7]

Without a well-built scaffold, visitors, like museum trustees, may get stalled, even before they enter. In fact, there's a term for this: threshold anxiety.[8]

As it was in 1989, so it remains in 2015: visitors want to be informed, yet they continue to feel intimidated in the museum's hallowed halls. Of course, there are many things we have learned since that time.

We now know that visitors don't all come to museums with the same sublime, existential goal in mind. After decades of research interviewing museum visitors, learning theorist John Falk suggests that visitors come with a wide variety of motivations, including an encounter with the sublime or the unfamiliar to be sure, but also the desire to check a "must-see" off their trip list or to simply have a good time with family or friends. Falk postulates that these motivations influence why people do many activities—not just visit museums. In fact, he states:

> What separates those who go to museums from those who do not is not whether they possess one of these . . . basic categories of need, but rather whether they perceive museums as places that satisfy these needs.[9]

Falk's message that some people perceive that museums will meet their needs while many others don't (and go elsewhere) is crucial; he has compared museums to asymmetrical bridges, where the side devoted to collection care is meticulously engineered, while the other side, the one that connects to the visitors, is only half-finished.

In 1988, the Field Museum published *Open Conversations: Strategies for Professional Development in Museums*, the fruit of six years of interactions with 500 museum professionals from more than 300 institutions.[10] In words that now seem prescient, that report stated:

> The growth of electronic forms of communication, the advent of new kinds of family units, and the ever-accelerating pace of modern life are among the conditions that influence people's perceptions and beliefs. Many museums have responded by developing exhibits and programs that better accommodate "where people are."

... Now the issues of museum education—and the language we use to characterize them—have begun to encompass the more inclusive notion of *visitor experience*.[11]

The report proceeded to outline the team approach, both in tongue-in-cheek stereotypes and in more productive terms, and it proposed three models that we have seen applied in the museums we have studied: cross-departmental working groups with either a content specialist, an audience specialist, or a process specialist as the leader.[12]

Of course, since the late 1980s, much progress has been made, especially in museums of natural science and history. Many history, natural science, and discovery museums have remade their approach, conceiving and executing exhibitions along the lines described in the Field book and successfully modeled for decades by San Francisco's Exploratorium.

Today, many point to the power of technology to connect, particularly in reaching a younger generation. Multimedia has been a powerful tool to restore the contexts the white cube galleries strip away, especially when it is placed in proximity to the objects on view. We have seen how devices like a mobile tour, app, or film clip allow an artist to talk directly about just what they were trying to do when putting those stones on the gallery floor, or a curator to let us know why an artist would paint canvas after canvas in just one color. But technology only goes so far—and can also provide an alibi to museum leaders or institutions who want limited change: *Yes, we're supplying all that information if you just take the audio tour or look at our website.* The sobering fact is the vast majority of museum visitors don't take the audio tour—or consult the museum's website.[13] What are we doing for them? It is incumbent on museums to reach those who don't choose to opt in to technology platforms during their museum visit.

The moment to connect with visitors is just-in-time: when they're in front of an object. If we can't count on technology to do the job, what about a person? More and more museums are experimenting with either replacing or supplementing their in-gallery security personnel with gallery attendants who know something about the objects on view and are encouraged to respond to visitor questions and engage them in conversations. This extension of the museum guard's vocation beyond simple asset protection holds great promise, as gallery attendants are typically the only museum staff with whom our visitors come into contact when they are in the galleries. Institutions ranging from the Phillips Collection in Washington, DC, to Tate Modern, the Walker Art Center, and the San Jose Museum of Art have seen fit to hire art students or artists to work in their galleries. The Guggenheim has adopted a hybrid solution, employing gallery guides to converse casually with visitors about the art even as they retain their traditional guard staff. Alternatively, at SITE Santa Fe, a contemporary art space in New Mexico, the gallery attendants have been trained in Visual Thinking Strategies in order to facilitate visitors' interactions with a changing array of cutting edge contemporary art.[14]

When a gallery guide is not present, the question becomes: What do we provide for our visitors? How do our buildings—and our gallery installations themselves—tell the stories of the objects we exhibit to anyone who arrives at any time? Finally, another important question surfaces, one of institutional mission: as professionals, do we have the will to make these concerns central to the way we welcome our visitors?

Key Takeaways

1. The prestige and authority museums enjoy in our culture come with a downside: many potential audiences see them as intimidating and exclusionary.
2. Museum objects rarely speak for themselves; the work of interpretation is "to provide hooks for the hookless."
3. A wave of audience research and museum reform efforts in the late 1980s led to transformation in many history and science museums but left art museums largely untouched.
4. Technology alone is not enough to make museums user friendly.

Notes

1 Naturalist and heritage interpretation pioneer Freeman Tilden understood interpretation as a *provocation*.
2 For example, in a recent SFMOMA audience study of culturally active Bay Area residents, 78% of potential visitors self-identified as having low-medium art knowledge, while 22% self-identified as high. SFMOMA and Wolff-Olins. *Insights + Persona Overview*. San Francisco: 2013. Internal document.
3 First published in Freeman Tilden, 1957/1977.
4 Alan Newman. "Report: What Did the Focus Groups Reveal?" In Getty Center for Education in the Arts and J. Paul Getty Museum, *Insights: Museums, Visitors, Attitudes, Expectations: A Focus Group Experiment*. Malibu, CA: J. Paul Getty Trust, 1991, pp. 112–122.
5 Research from the Minneapolis Institute of Arts rated the following categories of information as most helpful: subject/content; function; cultural and historical context; why the work is considered art and why it's in the museum; the artist; the technique; and, finally, economics—the value. Kris Wetterlund. "If You Can't See It, Don't Say It: A New Approach to Interpretive Writing." *Museum-Ed*. http://www.museum-ed.org/a-guide-to-interpretive-writing-about-art-for-museum-educators/ Accessed September 27, 2014.
6 Other findings that continue to resonate today: "The most common complaint was that the type was not big enough," and "The presence of guards actually reduced comfort for some visitors and increased intimidation for many first-time visitors."
7 Mihalyi Csikszentmihalyi. "Notes on Art Museum Experiences." In Getty Center for Education in the Arts and J. Paul Getty Museum, *Insights: Museums, Visitors, Attitudes, Expectations: A Focus Group Experiment*. Malibu, CA: J. Paul Getty Trust, 1991, pp. 123–131.

8 Elaine Heumann Gurian. "Threshold Fear." In *Civilizing the Museum: The Collected Writings of Elaine Heumann Gurian*. London and New York: Routledge, 2006.

9 John Falk. "The Museum Experience: Who Visits, Why and to What Effect?" Reprinted In Gail Anderson (Ed.), *Reinventing the Museum: The Evolving Conversation on the Paradigm Shift*. Lanham: AltaMira Press; 2nd Edition, 2012, pp. 317–329.

10 Research underwritten by the W.K. Kellogg Foundation.

11 Carolyn P. Blackmon, Teresa K. LaMaster, Lisa C. Roberts, and Beverly Serrell. *Open Conversations: Strategies for Professional Development in Museums*. Chicago: Field Museum of Natural History, 1988.

12 The insights in this book have been updated more recently by Polly McKenna-Cress and Janet Kamien in their 2014 book, *Creating Exhibitions*, a process manual for team-based exhibition development.

13 "Across the sector, a take-up rate of around 3 percent for permanent-collection audio guides is standard." Shelley Mannion, Amalia Sabiescu, and William Robinson. "An audio state of mind: Understanding behaviour around audio guides and visitor media." *MW2015: Museums and the Web 2015*. Published February 1, 2015. http://mw2015.museumsandtheweb.com/paper/an-audio-state-of-mind-understanding-behviour-around-audio-guides-and-visitor-media/ Accessed August 16, 2015.

14 Ted Loos. "Hi, Let's Talk Art. No, Really, It's My Job." *The New York Times*, August 6, 2006. http://www.nytimes.com/2006/08/06/college/coll06loos.html Accessed March 1, 2015.

2 Change Takes Leadership
Moments of Personal Transformation

Change begins with a recognition that something is not working or with the contrast of seeing something else work better. Museum veterans shared stories with us of how they suddenly came to see change as necessary. They described "Aha!" moments of personal transformation when they realized their museums were falling short of connecting with visitors. But in truth, none of these "Aha!" moments really happened overnight. While a flash of recognition can appear in an instant, understanding that change is needed comes from years of experience.

Perhaps because of their longevity, the three museum directors profiled below came to understand the need for change in a deep and personal way. Though it was never an easy undertaking, each director brought comprehensive change both to the organizational structure and to the forms of interpretation found in their galleries.

What precipitated this call to change? How did it play out? Three different stories emerge.

A Former Curator Moves beyond the Old Art History

The story of one destination museum's transformation is also a story of how a one-time curator, now museum director, came to see change as essential. Talking about the traditional museum approach, Detroit Institute of Arts Director Graham Beal begins by recounting that museums have become habituated to doing their job in a certain way. He describes the traditional museum job as "telling the story of art" and garnering large exhibition attendance. He goes on to explain how a reliance on information about art history has long been the gold standard for educating the public. Whether the focus is on Renaissance, Baroque, or even Contemporary objects, the approach has been similar: curators select and plan the exhibitions and catalogues and often write the wall text and labels as well. At the end, often as a last minute consideration, they educate the educators, who then translate the content of the exhibition in programming for the public. Although educators or interpretive specialists draw on research as well as information from interactions with the public, their expertise, if used at all, has typically been invoked post facto, once the exhibition has been fully installed.

While this traditional, curatorially driven model appropriately values the training and expertise of the art historians and curators, its focus is on objects, not those who view them. This model assumes that art historians and curators are also experts about audience, even though that is rarely the case. In fact, in what is perhaps a hallmark of their scholarly training, curators' love of their subject sometimes completely obscures their attention to the public.

Director Beal even suggests that art museums go beyond benignly overlooking their publics: they go so far as to alienate them. Talking about listening in on a visitor focus group, he notes: "But just the things that they said reinforced, more than anything else, how expert we are, actually, in pushing people away from the art, rather than engaging them."

Beal suggests that layering too much information pushes the public away because few visitors go to museums looking for lessons in art history. That does not mean that visitors lack the desire to understand the story or context behind objects. Rather, the "interpretive deficit"—the gap between an expert's intended meanings and what the audience takes away—challenges us to share our knowledge in more relevant ways and to better meet our visitors "where they are."

Trained in art history and a former curator himself, Beal had been unaware of the barriers that so many untrained visitors confront. His moment of clarity came years ago in a different museum. In that instance, the museum had addressed one audience hurdle—difficult language—by rewriting texts used to describe the exhibition.

> And that was really the penny that dropped for me, was when . . . we redid an installation—of the American and the European collections—and it didn't make any difference. The language was simpler and terminology was downplayed. But basically, we were still telling the story of Renaissance, Baroque, Rococo, and Neoclassicism. That is one way in.

Beal recognized that using simpler language was not enough to make audiences connect with what they were seeing. This "one way in" was still leaving out many audience members. Observing docent training further highlighted the problem. Beal says,

> I began to understand what a big gap there was, and that people who wanted to be docents were genuinely puzzled by what we were teaching . . . I now see that these people loved art; they came and they wanted to learn more about why they loved art; and what we did was to turn them into little art historians . . . but you're not drawn to art so you can learn art history; you're drawn to art because it has meaning, and a human meaning . . . I'd realized that we needed to get beyond the old art history.

He realized that if even docents, who were volunteering because of their love of art, were not connecting with the museum's content, there must be a problem in what and how information was being shared. He knew that the broader public must feel even more estranged. Beal came to see that there were gaps between the interests of art historians, museum staff, and the public.

The reaction of the docents suggested that attention to label writing was not enough; a whole new model for exhibition design was needed. Going beyond rewriting labels and crafting stories of art history would require new organizational processes and new voices. Graham Beal's realization led to a substantial structural change: the creation of new cross-departmental teams that included educators, exhibition designers, and evaluators, along with curators. Beal also intentionally included staff members completely unschooled in art to serve as stand-in surrogates for the public. The new teams were charged with a difficult task: coming up with a way to connect two worlds: that of museum professionals with that of the broader public. In addition, the teams were also charged with collaborating in a new way; curators were now working together on equal footing with colleagues from different departments who brought other forms of expertise. An open mind, patience, and an ability to listen well became added job requirements.

Beal asked his teams to keep in mind two important questions:

> "Why does this object exist?" As I say, somewhere, sometime, someone asked someone else to make something for some purpose. And then the second question is, "Why is it in the DIA?"

These questions were aimed at pushing the team beyond their assumptions about audience or art history to carve out new ways of connecting with the public. Searching for effective visitor-centered ideas, the staff benefited from working in new teams: now they were brainstorming with experts of different stripes, combining visitor questions, content design, and education, all in one mix.

The "Vision Keeper": Children Inspire a New Mission

For Lori Fogarty, being the Director of the Oakland Museum of California (OMCA) starts with articulating a vision and being a leader who drives an institution-wide agenda for change.

> I see myself as the vision keeper here . . . I saw an important part of my role was articulating the mission and the vision of the institution . . . And I had a similar sense, that my job was to be the facilitator of . . . major initiatives . . . to make happen, and kind of move them through the institution.

The importance of a visitor-centered approach crystallized for Fogarty when she moved from working in a major urban art museum to being the director of a children's discovery museum. She comments:

> It was a huge change of culture and vision and mission. And what I think I really learned there was to work in an institution that was truly all about the audience. It doesn't have a collection. The exhibition program is, you know, not at all like it is in an art museum or a collection-based institution. So really grounding myself in thinking about audience in a much deeper way. And also, children's museums are interdisciplinary, so it freed me to think about different aspects of particularly interdisciplinary or multidisciplinary programming.

Fogarty took to heart the lessons she learned from working with children as she came to understand the importance of audience in a whole new way. Without a focus on exhibition objects, her time in a discovery museum also allowed her to experiment with collection-free ways of engaging audiences. When she assumed the directorship of OMCA, with its combination of natural history, history, and art collections, she retained her visitor-centered focus:

> I think what really changed for me over the last few years was . . . to be at the heart of really identifying and articulating and espousing this very strong visitor-centered focus in this project. And not just this project now, everything the museum does.

While all museums have mission statements, few fully commit to making them real. However, over several years Fogarty's new visitor-centered mission became the driving force behind a complete museum overhaul. With the help of outside grants, the OMCA completely restructured its organization from the ground up: rewriting job descriptions, adding new hires, encouraging some staff to leave, and having those who remained work in newly configured cross-departmental teams. Along with the dramatic organizational changes came bold visitor-focused interpretive components, such as roving gallery guides, introductory texts in multiple languages, colored walls, comfortable seating, and a range of in-gallery interactive activities. These ways of welcoming the public became the OMCA's new norm.

For Lori Fogarty and her museum, being visitor-centered has become a comprehensive philosophy, impacting every decision and every corner of the museum.

Meaningful Spaces That Go beyond an Idealized Visitor

The visitor-centered change we encountered in some US museums is happening in many other places where strong leadership reigns. In Europe we encountered another leader: Glasgow Museum's Mark O'Neill. His commitment to audience reflects a social system where arts and culture are as important for community enrichment as are sports or education.

O'Neill talks about his roots:

> I had worked in a community museum for five years. And I suppose I had worked out my philosophy there, which was about making museum space meaningful for people. . . . So I suppose my basic philosophy is about engaging the public by finding the things that are most deep and meaningful to them in the collections on display.

His perspective on audience first evolved when he was working in a community museum; when he moved to the much larger Kelvingrove Art Gallery and Museum, with collections incorporating art, history, and natural history, this didn't change.

> I learned how to elaborate my views, in relation to everything from art to arms and armor, to natural history . . . We tried to say what the objects meant to the people who made them, not what the curatorial discipline thought was interesting.

Seeing visitors as central, O'Neill goes on to connect maker stories with visitor interests. Audience research helped the museum better understand the interests of actual visitors.

> I suppose the big addition [in Kelvingrove] . . . was visitor studies. So very much about deepening an understanding of people who might visit museums, very much trying to move away from an idealized visitor . . .
>
> There's a kind of an imaginary aesthetic visitor, solitary male, no friends, no family. They are scarcely even able to go to the toilet.

Without the benefit of research to fully understand the profile of different visitors, a mistaken, idealized, imaginary visitor can easily appear. Research can quickly dispel these idealized notions, replacing them with more realistic portraits. For O'Neill, this broader understanding of audience naturally leads to an interest in new ideas, often associated with the consistently underrepresented groups who are now making their way to the museum.

In this light, confronting controversial subjects in the exhibitions—or as he says, "challenging received wisdom"—does not appear as much of a departure. Taking on difficult topics such as violence against women and sectarianism in the city's showplace museum has not been easy, and O'Neill has faced his share of critics. But these objections have not stopped O'Neill or his successors from tackling real and important subjects.

O'Neill's ultimate goal was to create a rich, multifunctional space that appeals to a broad demographic who see themselves reflected in its halls and essential to its conversations.

> It mightn't have succeeded, but we wanted it to be beautiful. And we wanted it to have spiritual places, contemplative. I mean, it was big enough to do everything; to appease people and to have reflection and excitement, and we tried to do all that. I mean, museums are really unusual. . . . I think they're probably the only medium that has to cover the whole age range, whole demographic . . . So we tried to base that on the reality of how people are, not on some sort of abstract notion of an idealized visitor.

O'Neill's focus on the reality of "how people are" also leads to including new voices that grow from this fuller understanding of the museum's audience. He makes a distinction between "insider" and "outsider" voices. The Insider Voice is that of the traditional museum professionals who have assumed that their take on objects is sufficient. The Outsider Voice, comprising the expanded audience, is often not heard. For O'Neill, a model that focuses principally on the Insider Voice is inadequate. Mere inclusion of an Outsider Voice alone is not enough. He describes the importance of an "insider-outsider dialogue" in a museum he developed, one devoted to world religions:

> And it was a mixture of voices. The curatorial voice was there, and the curator did choose what they thought was interesting or important; but also, there were the voice[s] of believers. So the insider-outsider dialogue. I don't particularly like museums that are all insider museums, inside-voice museums.

This approach incorporates a curatorial voice and expertise but does not stop there. It adds the voices of others who are not always included. When a broader audience participates in the dialogue, we get a chance to share more varied sources of knowledge and expression.

To enact this audience-centric vision, O'Neill's team took on a highly ambitious multi-year project that transformed both the museum's exhibitions and the way staff worked. For example, in the galleries they added interpretation and activities geared for families, such as works of art hung at child-height or tables with games. They produced exhibits using objects drawn from across collections (a sword and an armadillo) to address complex subjects like armaments and war. Organizationally, they shook things up by adding new job titles and team configurations. In an uncommon move, they also made objects available for closer inspection at an off-site facility where the public can make an appointment to handle or see objects up close, 361 days a year.

Criticized by many in the museum world as catering to the lowest common denominator, the museum nonetheless appears to remain a big hit with the local community who flock to its free halls—and return again and again, appreciating it as a valued community resource. Though not without its problems, Kelvingrove stands as a leader innovating with a bold visitor-centered vision.

Key Takeaways

In this section, we present the transformative paths taken by three seasoned museum directors:

1. Graham Beal realized that the traditional approach of many museum professionals holds little or no meaning for others and is simply not good enough.
2. Lori Fogarty's work in a collection-free children's museum, where it's all about audience, results in a restructured organization and bold new interpretive components.
3. Having worked in community museums, Mark O'Neill continues to focus on what is meaningful to his audience. Visitor studies show him that an idealized visitor does not exist. Once the idealized is replaced with the real, new audiences and issues arise. These challenges only expand the museum's opportunity to serve—and to thrive.

3 Contours of Change

Moving forward, we look at some of the institutional changes taking place as museums incorporate visitor-centered approaches. Having already heard how three leaders decided to initiate change, we now see the impact of these new ideas.

We hear about the challenges that curators, educators, and others face—including new power dynamics, turf wars, even resistance to change. Not to minimize the complexities involved, we offer directors' perspectives regarding their own mixed feelings. We also highlight the benefits many professionals feel as new opportunities emerge and visitors are more engaged.

Finally, hinting at the more developed cases to come in Part II, we conclude this section with three brief case studies—models of change that suggest new and creative ways forward.

Changing Models: New Teams Emerge

> "Is it possible to do your job [and] at the same time rethink the job?"
> —Curator Christiane Berndes, Van Abbe Museum

While attending to visitors does not inherently require that organizations revise work processes or traditional hierarchies, in our small study this was often the case. Unexpectedly and repeatedly, we saw museum professionals working together in new configurations. The precise make-up and leadership of teams varied, but multiple disciplines were always represented. Importantly, a flattened or altered hierarchy was a hallmark of these new teams.

We also saw teams with new leaders. Some teams were co-led by curators and educator/interpretive specialists, others by project managers, and still others by a new position title: Experience Designers. However, none of the teams was led by a curator alone. Inclusion of educators as team leaders may make sense, given that listening to visitors' perspectives has always been an integral part of the educator's job. In other words, prioritizing visitors as essential to the museum mission may also lead to empowering the voices of those who have traditionally had most direct contact with them.

We witnessed educators, curators, and other team members increasingly working together as peers and bringing their different realms of expertise to the table.

As they respond to a new visitor-oriented mission, museum directors have adopted a range of organizational strategies: from creating new job titles or job descriptions to new work processes and new kinds of teams. In one case, we saw fundamental change that involved reinventing the entire organizational structure of the museum from the ground up.

New Power Dynamics

While organizational change impacts everyone, often it can appear most threatening to curators. In fact, the threat to curators is a theme we noticed repeatedly in our interviews. This issue was voiced by directors and educators, as well as by curators themselves. Perhaps because curators already have power within the museum and see themselves as designated guardians of the collections, they struggle most with diminished control. When organizational changes redistribute authority more evenly across departments, some curators fear they are losing their mandate and become unsure of their evolving role.

An American museum director recounts his conversations with skeptical colleagues, including a director in Europe, about how curators are handling change:

> I can think of two directors—one in Europe and one over here—who, when I said what I was doing, both basically asked the question, Why are the curators allowing this? . . . That was basically it. How are you dealing with the curators? It's symptomatic of a huge change.

Asking a fellow director how he is "dealing with the curators" gives some indication of the significance of the changes afoot.

One curator talks about how shifts in power also reflect a shift in funding.

> I would say it's such a big shift, for those of us that have been around for a long time. But within museums, power was always—the intellectual power, the kind of muscle, the decision-making power, obviously, was with the director. But the director, I think, was always more aligned with curators. . . . And I really think the funding model has changed dramatically. So now, there's so much more grant money, research money, foundation money, going to education.

Whether or not this curator is right about how new education funding is driving some of the change, the salient point is that educators and other team members are being included early on, often in new leadership roles. As the curator acknowledges, new power dynamics are evident, including a possible realignment of museum directors with different team members. Regardless of which alliances are foremost, shifts in power are taking place.

Reactions and Concerns

It is perhaps not surprising that some curators are concerned enough to actively thwart the very changes exemplified by the museums profiled in this book. A director of a destination museum talks about a curator he perceived as obstructionist: "We have one curator I pulled off a team because he was sabotaging it, basically . . . sort of foot dragging and that kind of thing." This kind of reluctance on the part of curators was not an isolated instance.

In fact, the Association of Art Museum Curators (AAMC) was founded in 2002 "in response to news of staff re-organizations at several major US museums," and in part to actively combat what was perceived as the erosion of curatorial authority within the museum field.[1] The AAMC's Strategic Plan for 2009–2012 prescribed an advocacy posture. Priorities included: increasing exposure and building public recognition for curators; curatorial promotion and advancement; and recruitment and expansion of member rolls within the organization itself. There was no mention of reaching across the aisle to collaborate as equals with other museum staff, or of the importance of audience or visitors.

Dumbing Down

Some curators worry that the museum's standards of scholarship may be at risk, along with the kind of work for which they were trained and on which the museum's collection-building depends. Coming both from internal staff and outside colleagues or critics, accusations of "dumbing down" loom large. After a significantly more visitor-centered gallery reinstallation, a museum director talks about this kind of attack:

> As soon as word got out, there were nothing but attacks, based on the idea of dumbing down and Disneyfication. "Well, I haven't heard anything yet, but it certainly sounds like dumbing down to me." And it's perfect: "I haven't seen anything yet, but it's going to be terrible."

The director notes how accusations of dumbing down come almost automatically—sometimes even before a critic has set foot in the exhibit. A curator echoes tales of outside critics who begin with automatic criticism. In one case a critic went even further, first criticizing the exhibit, then later hailing it as a benchmark.

Anticipating accusations of dumbing down, another museum director speaks honestly of concerns about how their new exhibit will be viewed. "I don't want people to think we're dumbing down an experience. I think we're about opening up new points of entry for people. But I think we are in a big period of change and there is going to be a lot of tension for a while."

While not happy with comments about dumbing down, the director knows that change is difficult and often comes with criticism. These leaders persevere even as they anticipate critical attacks.

Turf Wars

Several directors noted how label writing is now a place where tensions about authority play out. Often this conflict is between the curators and educators. Label writing has become the testing ground for working out new ideas as well as new types of relationships.

What follows are excerpts from museum directors sharing candid stories about label writing turf wars. To emphasize the pervasiveness of these skirmishes, we share multiple examples.

One museum director comments:

> And I'm sure you've heard before that it really was all symbolized by the labels: who took authorship of the labels. So the credit I take is for having the power to make sure that the new ideas were retained and not swamped or perverted . . . But [the curators] resisted to the end, and the labels really did become a symbol of loss of control of their public spaces.

As the director suggests, label writing has become related to control of territory and perhaps more importantly, of museum voice. Ultimately this director intervenes to ensure that the new ideas and ways of working don't get derailed. In our study, we commonly saw museum directors intervening in these kinds of disputes. Another museum director also talks frankly about curators rankling under new practices that they perceive as a threat to their authority:

> One of the curators—it was so far into the process I couldn't believe we were even having the conversation. But he said, "You know, I don't understand why this is so complicated. We just used to write the labels and we put them up. Why do we have to do this?" You know? . . . And so it plays out in a lot of little ways. And giving up that power and authority . . . is not easy. It's not easy for people.

While the director understands the challenges staff face as roles and authority shift, he is surprised about the reluctance of a curator to adapt to the museum's new cooperative label writing process. The new label writing approach was put in place because the old labels had too much jargon and were simply not reaching the visitors. The fact that some museums have resorted to farming their "voice" out to freelance writers—often with a journalism degree—reflects directors' understanding that traditional museum practice and today's audiences have drifted far apart. It is also a strategy used by directors to overcome internal strife over labels. While directors are sympathetic about how difficult the process might be for some staff, they are also ready to take control as needed. This is a very delicate line to tread: the desire to honor professional staff with years of training, on the one hand, and a new visitor-centered mandate that requires bold changes that sometimes feel threatening to those involved, on the other.

Clearly articulating new visitor-centered priorities, one museum director talks frankly about how a label-writing power struggle played out: based on research and testing, new, larger white labels were designed. Without hesitation, he states his own bottom line:

> The simplest example is that a couple of the curators and a couple of critics, who liked the overall effect, objected to the large white labels on the walls. You know, "Why didn't you tone them down? Why didn't you use a similar color?" Well, the answer really was, we had learned that people miss them. People don't read them. They're harder to read, so people don't read them. Whereas in the old days, aesthetics would definitely have won. And in this case, it was, Okay, this is what suits the general visitor and it's too bad if someone's aesthetic sensibility is wounded a little bit. That's not the priority. It's the comfort and the ease for the visitor.

As the director makes clear, outcomes shift when visitors' needs take center stage. The museum has a new approach: when it comes to designing labels, audience research trumps aesthetics. In our study, all the directors were willing to articulate a new bottom line. In fact, a willingness to hold that bottom line proves to be an essential aspect of leadership for change.

War Stories

While change may be necessary, even when embraced it is rarely easy. One museum director compares the process to being cast off in a lifeboat surrounded by lightning:

> We pushed off from the shore in a lifeboat. We couldn't see land. It was thundering and rain—You know, it was lightning and storming. The water was lapping up over the edges. Now, not only can we see land, we're hitting the beach.

Hinting at the rigors involved in change, a curator who favored working in such newly created cross-functional teams refers to getting a "battlefield promotion." In fact, metaphors of battle, like "protecting territory" or "sabotage," are common when museum staff talk about the process of change. This is true of directors, educators, and curators. A museum director comments, "We have skirmishes in doing special exhibitions." This unfiltered language reveals the challenges and deeply felt struggles of those involved. Staff willingly share their "war stories"—whether of complete or partial institutional transformation.

Loss

Sharing deep knowledge and a love of art or historical objects, museum directors, like their colleagues, also share an anxiety about disturbing the sacrosanct exhibition or museum environment. They too appreciate a pure art encounter.

As a one-time curator herself, one director understands the difficulties faced by curators and reveals her personal feelings as she talks about mourning the loss of the pure art experience:

> For curators, I think this is hard. I really, really do. And I have to tell you, there are days, still, when the old museum world of the kind of pure spaces—There's a missing of that, for me. You know? I mean, I think you mourn something—I think there's a continually mourning and reinventing. I mean, I think if you don't own up to the mourning part, you're not really ready to forge into the future.

One museum director shared a chart her consultant had provided her, adapted from Kübler-Ross's Stages of Grief (Figure 3.1).

The chart illustrates the struggles and sense of loss encountered by teams creating change. A Danger Zone occurs at Stage 3, when staff is still having a hard time releasing the old model and may well be losing faith that any good will come of all this effort. Their old ways of working can no longer be relied upon and the benefits of the new system are not yet visible. This is a tough time—before the dawn of more permanent systems—when museum teams must stay the course. Change continues throughout: even at Stage 6, Integration, fine-tuning is still taking place. We are reminded that change, like loss, has its distinct stages and continues on. There is no real end, no steady state.

One director shares her surprise at the internal resistance and even hostility she found among trustees and faithful patrons when she tested new ways of reaching a broader audience.

> But one of the things I wasn't anticipating in this journey was having to help that core audience be okay with other tools that help a broader public. They often feel hostile to those tools or they're anxious about those tools or they feel those tools are disrupting the art experience.

The director was caught off guard, wrongly assuming that those who loved the art as much as she did would want to share it with members of the community who had been too intimidated to visit.

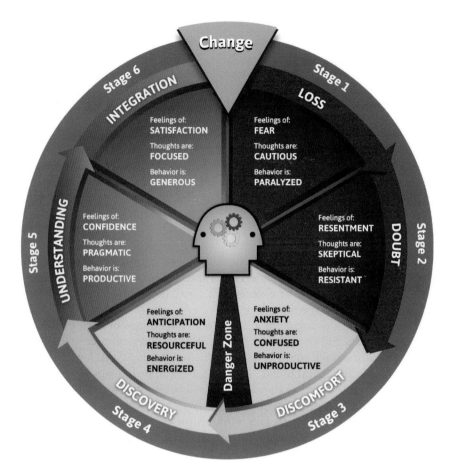

Figure 3.1 The Change Cycle. Courtesy www.changecycle.com

The French sociologist of culture, Pierre Bourdieu (1930–2002), would not have been surprised by this counter-reaction. It was Bourdieu who, in a succession of books written from the 1960s into the 1990s, suggested that high art masquerades as a universal language but is really the production of economic and intellectual forces geared to preserving distinctions of social class. That is why its language feels so secret to some but natural to others. Academics, professionals, artists, and the monied classes are exposed to high culture—be it visual or performing arts, music or literature—throughout their education to the point that it becomes part of their identity. This taste or breeding is what Bourdieu dubbed "social capital"—a set of shared references, gleaned from critics, authorities, and sheer purchasing power. A museum that seeks to overcome these perceived "barriers to entry" and welcome new visitors—outsiders—has its work cut out for itself. In some sense, Bourdieu is the ghost haunting these pages.[2]

A Gap in Understanding

Some exhibits seem geared more to colleagues than a broader public. For example, one director talks frankly about a curator including more objects than the public could appreciate.

> You know, like twice as many eighteenth century ceramics in a case as is needed. But of course, the curators, they want the maroon and the yellow and the green example. You know, that's great to them; we should show my colleagues that I've got all of this. And of course, most people look at a crowded case and say, "Oh, I can't deal with that," and just turn around.

In a similar vein, another director talks about reminding a curator that since there were already 331 objects in a show, there was no need to worry about replacing two of those objects with a wall text that explained why the objects were there in the first place.

These observations highlight a gap in understanding—or even purpose—between experts and the general public. While experts appreciate the fine details that distinguish similar objects in their collections, this level of attention is lost on the general public. Museums have to be judicious in their collection presentations unless they are prepared to go the extra mile in sharing their expert knowledge in useful ways.

Increasingly, museum directors, with visitors on their radar, understand this problem and are better prepared to address it. As one sympathetic curator says:

> If the public doesn't engage with the holdings of a museum, what is the purpose of a museum? There's academia, there's safety deposit vaults in banks. I don't think that a museum is a bank or a safety deposit box.

Such comments point to a larger debate going on within museum walls. Whether in the guise of pared-down information, number of objects on display, or where and when information (not to mention seating) should be made available, the debate often boils down to considering the importance of reaching, even recruiting, a broader audience. For many insiders, providing broader access is seen as having too high a cost—with the value of a pure art encounter or even a worthwhile museum visit itself at stake.

Some museum veterans (particularly in art museums) feel strongly that the goal of reaching out to visitors is misguided. They value a more traditional display of objects and look for other ways to involve the public that do not impact the galleries (i.e., event-based programming, Friday evening cocktails, etc.). For some, a permanent gallery-based focus on audience is simply seen as outside the museum mandate.

Terry Smith, an Australian critic, has written extensively about problems of contemporary curating. He says:

> Interpretation remains in the wings, a second order of knowledge, awaiting the viewer who is imagined standing in front of the work in the context of an exhibition staged by the curator . . . Within the space of the exhibition itself, the curator's interpretation remains unstated, implicit. In its explicit form, it usually becomes available to the viewer later—in the catalogue, for example, as a supplement.[3]

The notion of a museum viewer faced with implicit information is all too familiar. Asking the public to figure things out on their own or seek out a catalogue in order to understand an exhibit is asking a lot. After all, how many members of the public are going to go out of their way to secure a catalogue for an exhibition to which they haven't connected in the first place?

Ironically, a big advantage that history and science museums have over art museums is that they *know* they have to add context—and have no taboo against doing so. In the words of museum veteran Scott Sayre:

> Art starts in a messy, physical, emotional environment and ends up in a sterile, clean room environment with little or no evidence of the human aspect of its creation. Science museums, on the other hand, often deal with complex, highly controlled work, developed in a clean room environment, which ends up being exhibited in a highly interactive, physically engaging, social environment.[4]

Regardless of their origins, all objects need some kind of interpretive support. In fact, we in art museums are disingenuous when we say we believe in the pure art experience for all. As a matter of course, we give trustees and collectors preferential access to curator tours and brief them privately on the background and import of the art on view. We would never dream of *not* advising this vital patron constituency: leaving them alone and potentially feeling puzzled—or worse yet, alienated—without a guiding hand.

Yet when it comes to the greater public, many museums—and art museums in particular—are fine with leaving them adrift. In the words of Denver Art Museum veteran Marlene Chambers, "To assume an inherent stupidity in those who do not already know the information we have spent a lifetime acquiring only reveals our own narrow-mindedness."[5] If the art speaks for itself, why did we go to school and get advanced degrees to understand it?

The pretense that art or objects speak for themselves is not sustainable. As in any area of study, whether physics or, for our purposes, art history, expertise is earned, so why wouldn't museums need to supplement a visitor's ability to decipher the codes embedded in that training?

Closing the Gap

One director recounts a conversation that revealed the distance she had already traveled:

> I did have this incredible conversation with a very significant contemporary artist . . . I realized that the anxiety that she was expressing was similar to the anxiety and viewpoint that I think I had coming into this, which is that she believes that a good or great art object . . . can transcend any barriers and communicate directly with the viewer; that it needs no facilitation; and that that facilitation—Not only is the facilitation unneeded or unnecessary, the facilitation can be obstructionist, can obstruct the experience and create sort of a noise, a white noise that interferes.
>
> I realized that I don't believe that anymore. I believed it at one point in my life, clearly. And I do believe, for a certain subset of our audience, that that is true. They do not need any of those things. Because this is something that deeply interests them, they come with a lot of knowledge . . . they know the arc of art history. . . . They're used to slowing down, looking deeply, having thoughts while they're looking. And that's a core audience for us—I don't want to alienate that audience.

Such comments reveal the deeper understanding shared by directors, many of whom began as curators. Understanding that experts often do not require or even want further information in the galleries, she does not want to alienate that peer group. But, as a museum director and advocate, she also recognizes that most people are not privy to this kind of art or museum experience.

As keepers of culture, these and other directors have come to embrace a broader sense of responsibility and desire to engage the public. In the meantime, while directors continue to offer special treatment to their Trustees and top patrons—treatment that these supporters have come to expect—they must also explain to them their vision for a museum that "means more, to more people, than ever before."

Benefits of Change

Of course, not all curators feel threatened or resist change. Talking about what she has gained from working in a new team, Christiane Berndes, curator of collections at the Van Abbe Museum, talks about her own growth:

> And I think this helps people to open up, because it's all about daring to question what you're doing. And daring to . . . listen to suggestions of the other, to rethink what you are doing. . . . Especially with people

in different fields, because you often have to explain things that are so clear for you. Why do they ask for this? But the question might open up—It might make you rethink—Because you don't know what you don't know.

As the curator reflects, listening anew to questions colleagues pose can reveal what you know or don't. Working with others across disciplines forces you to explain things clearly. As most teachers know, the process of explaining can bring with it a new sense of clarity and new insights for the participants themselves.

Several curators talk about their pride in the achievement of the group and even credit the educators for helping shape their new way of thinking. One says: "I feel so proud of the work we've done . . . I thank our educators every day, because they have turned me into a new kind of thinker."

While new team configurations can be challenging, the excitement of seeing visitors linger in the galleries, having a discussion or even losing track of time, is not lost on those who spend their lives devoted to the museum and its treasures. One museum director simply marks his visitor-centered success by the reduction of hate mail he receives. He says:

> I don't get hate mail. I don't get any hate mail. The mail I get is mail that people express their pleasure at having been at the [museum]. But my mail, which for my whole career has been ten to one unfavorable experiences to favorable, is completely the other way around.

A curator who co-led a team with an interpretive specialist and who likes the new configuration talks about how the approach to working together has changed:

> The model shifted from, you know, educators being kind of the last tag-on thing that we did to being more fully integrated into the conversation. We kept making it earlier and earlier—which is, of course, the other lesson we learned. And now it's just common practice.

The curator's statement highlights an important aspect of the change: timing. Rather than educators only being included at the end of planning, directors now mandate that they are present from the outset. This builds in educators' input all along the way, and attests to the new emphasis on visitor experience. Being included early on also ensures that needed resources are allocated up front. Now the whole team not only jointly considers the ideas; they also decide together on resource allocation—time and money—to make things happen. Having resources at the ready to back up the new ideas can go a long way toward creating a new approach. This is indeed a sign of progress—and evidence of precisely the kind of innovation we are advocating in this book.

Perhaps sharing visitor data is where new efforts need to be focused. Terry Smith pinpoints a museum behavior that might seem counterintuitive:

> It is disappointing that there is so scant a record of audience responses to art exhibitions. Curators talk about it all the time as the holy grail of their profession but do very little . . . to actually examine it in depth and detail.[6]

What if we actually gave curators the data they need about what's connecting and what isn't?

Judy Rand, author of the "Visitor Bill of Rights" (reprinted on pages 5–6), talks about benefits of visitor data:

> A big part of my job is to bridge the gap between visitors and curators. Visitor research tells me how big the gap is. Visitor research tells me where my visitors are coming from, so I know what kind of bridge to build to get a message from us to them, and back again.[7]

As educators and directors have come to understand, looking at data can be eye opening, even mission changing. It's hard to know how much impact facing facts could really have on the field if universally considered.

There is another positive sign of change: in 2015, the AAMC's annual meeting included one panel on new technologies and curatorial practice, and concluded with another titled "Curatorial Practice and the Educational Turn." It explicitly addressed these questions:

- How is the curatorial role shifting or evolving in the education turn?
- What are constructive models for collaboration between curatorial and education in engaging audiences?
- How does interest in visitor experience and participatory projects impact the curatorial profession?
- How does the position of Engagement curator operate in an in-between state between curatorial, education, and audience?[8]

Reframing

Ultimately, what may be needed in the field is a reframing: seeing challenge as an opportunity. For many of the museum directors in our study, attending to the public is not seen as a trade-off, but as an opportunity for growth.

OMCA's Lori Fogarty shares her comprehensive perspective:

> It's not a trade-off. It's an *and*, not an *or*, to be visitor-centered and committed to scholarship, committed to collection care, committed to, you know, the primacy of the object, to the role of the artist. Yes, we still care about serious scholarship, we care about curatorial expertise. And in fact, visitors want that as well, you know?

That was part of our testing, they still are eager to see what the curators think and why the curators think this is important, and understand the substantive content, and be able to give their own perspective and tell their own story.

I think it opens you up to a lot more possibilities. . . . It doesn't diminish the expertise or authority, but it opens you up to whole new ways of thinking.

From these inclusive views, ones that allow for many voices and forms of expertise, there is room for audience in tandem with the traditional concerns of museum staff: attention to collection care, artist voice, historical context, and the importance of the object. In fact, we are reminded that visitors also want all these components and they depend on museums to supply the needed expertise.

Perhaps part of the challenge, then, is to find less threatening ways to include new voices. There is no reason to suggest that curators' deep knowledge about objects and art history is any less critical than in the past, but there is a need for other voices to be heard as well—not to mention that more and more audiences want to know how collections and exhibitions relate to *them*. Museum authority alone is of limited appeal to a public that increasingly sees itself as "curating" its own life. Including new colleagues who focus on audience as part of planning and exhibition design only adds to the museum's pool of knowledge and its ability to keep apace with changing times. However, recognizing this logic is a long way from actually implementing new approaches and welcoming fresh perspectives within the entrenched cultures of museum practice.

Three New Models

An Experience Designer Offers a Bridge

While not everyone agrees that prioritizing audience comes without trade-offs, new models—and new ways of working—may lessen these concerns. In fact, taking on the challenge of meeting the needs of multiple audiences can spur innovation. At the Van Abbe Museum in the Netherlands, we found a kind of hybrid position, "Experience Designer," a title now increasingly common in the museum field. Crafting new positions may be one innovative way to proceed. In this case, from the get-go, the job of the experience designer is to build bridges among curators, educators, and the public.

The experience designer Hadas Zemer Ben-Ari explains her role:

But what my position was, and still is, is a kind of bridge. Always, I was presented as the bridge. And I was not part of the curatorial team; I was part of the production, for the production-presentation team, because there was an understanding: Okay, if this is a creative house, then creatively thinking people are everywhere.

And that was a new thing, as well; to understand that this is not only the curators' work, but also this should happen in the other departments. But I had very good conversations and very good access to the curators. We could discuss together. Then I could bring that to the other departments, like the education department, the production department, and understand it's kind of a tuning, very much a tuning work, of what will work and what will not work and who needs to compromise where.

Designed from the outset as a bridge, the position incorporated sensitivity to the different parties and to the process itself, thus facilitating the "tuning" necessary for bringing in multiple voices. Tuning is important, as rarely does a system arrive fully ready. Tuning—defined here as attention to and refining of the process itself—invites the shaping of processes over time. In other words, attention to process acknowledges the necessary time and inherent complexities of bringing together different parties. This is important for staff as they grow into new roles. Creating a new position up front might allow a museum to grapple with these issues in a productive and non-threatening way.

Underlying the creation of the new position was an important emerging philosophy. Zemer describes some of the intellectual underpinnings of her position:

> I've acknowledged a gap between the very progressive work that the museum was [doing] . . . offering certain content in quite a radical way; but the experience that was offered to the visitors was very traditional. There was really a gap there. And that fascinated me.
>
> How can you bridge that gap? And how can you deliver your message without compromising it, but yet joining—joining more people to the conversation?

Given this position, Zemer could focus on intellectual problems rather than internal staff wrangling. Keeping an eye on shared problems or ideas may be a helpful way of reframing. The gap noted by this experience designer highlights the notion that a museum can be aesthetically radical—as some curators might consider themselves to be—while remaining quite conservative in its approach to audience. When institutions are not uniformly innovative, the unevenness presents an opportunity for growth.

As the experience designer understands, reframing challenges as joint opportunities might just lead to new creative approaches as well as better work relations.

A Visitor-Centric Curator Eager to Share His Interests

In another example, we see another new hire and new hybrid position—this time a curator is brought in who is already aligned with the director's visitor-centered initiative. Tasked with combining worlds, OMCA's René de

Guzman refers to himself as a "curator-educator hybrid, curator-marketer," evolving to fill a need. When asked how the position is evolving, he talks about how his work in the museum is in sync with his own interests. As a curator who trained as an artist, he does not feel at odds with prioritizing visitors:

> I think I'm staying true to my passions around art, and I try to explain this to other curators: If you love the stuff so much, wouldn't you want to share it? Just trying to find sort of enlightened self-interest. Don't you want to share it and build a really strong constituency around what you love?
>
> And that's how I feel, in terms of my work. I care about this stuff. I want to build a strong support for it and I want other people to understand why I love this stuff. And so that's where these sorts of hybridized functions come together. Because I care and believe in this stuff.

Brought on board to help lead the change, the curator is interested in sharing his love of art with the public. He is also critical of curatorial colleagues who don't share this view. They seem reluctant to change, and "create the situation where you deprive a lot of people of the resources and lose an opportunity to really create great experience."

This curator maintains a positive outlook, hoping to lead others by seeing what is possible, rather than focusing on problems that get in the way. While he is not blind to the difficult task of figuring out an effective way to share the art he loves with untrained visitors, he sees this as a worthy and exciting goal. Inspired to create "great experiences" for the public, he believes this is best done in collaboration with others.

Teams Working across Disciplines

A museum director focused on building more effective cross-disciplinary teams presents another example of how internal organizational change leads to a more visitor-centered outcome. Here the challenge is finding new ways to work with existing colleagues in new roles. This means learning to listen anew and work across disciplines.

The museum director discusses the challenges and the need for cross-translation:

> One of the challenges is trying to create new teams of people that are cross-disciplinary, that really listen to each other. That's hard, because people talk different languages. Even within an art museum context, education curators and educators talk a different language than the art curators, than the marketing people.

It's easy to assume that staff working together in a museum can readily communicate with each other, but in fact, this may not be true. Each siloed department or discipline may have its own terminology and assumptions that can get in the way of understanding. A director talks about how challenging it is for familiar colleagues to talk across language barriers. They often need new skills at speaking as well as at listening. The director continues:

> And naturally, one of the things that comes up is that we're talking across each other. So I think that getting people out of their comfort zone is the strategy. But then how do you help them feel okay? That's been the big strategy for us.

Trust-building exercises and workshops can help. Often, traveling together to see other visitor-focused museums—negotiating airport transfers and eating dinners together—provides the first opportunity for these professionals to get to know each other as people outside of their professional roles. Seeking to improve dialogue and change old habits of interaction, this director is interested in leveling the playing field; by including everyone at the table at the outset, she models more effective behavior and offers a new way of working. The goal is that staff members meet each other anew and redefine old patterns. No doubt, bringing everyone to the table as equals takes patience and leadership. Clearly, abandoning hierarchies doesn't come overnight. Moreover, in our experience, it does not happen without a director's direct involvement.

The three models of visitor-inspired change presented here offer only a few ideas of what is possible with creativity and teamwork.

An experience designer as a bridge: creating a position, defined as a bridge, helps staff work out differences and come together. The approach honors different staff views and allows time for curators and educators to find their own meaningful ways of working together.

An artist curator as leader: a curator who believes in sharing his love of art inspires others to find ways to reach a broader audience. Working together with new team members on a joint challenge is seen as a worthy goal.

Staff talking across disciplines: staff is urged to overcome traditional communication gulfs. By including everyone at the table from the outset, museum staff begins to meet on more equal footing and to develop improved models of working. Patience is needed as relations build.

Key Takeaways

1. With a new visitor-centered mandate, organizational change is unavoidable.
2. Power and control are up-ended, with curators losing top-dog status. Battle mentality can ensue.
3. Change is naturally a process: ongoing, messy, complex. It's both resisted and welcomed, but never easy.
4. Staff traditions and approaches can be reframed to let everyone buy in.

Notes

1 The Association of Art Museum Curators: Mission and History. http://www.art curators.org/?History Accessed September 27, 2014, and comments from DIA Director Graham Beal.
2 Pierre Bourdieu. *Distinction: A Social Critique of the Judgment of Taste.* Translated by Richard Nice. Cambridge: Harvard University Press, 1984.
3 Terry Smith. *Thinking Contemporary Curating.* New York: Independent Curators International, 2012, pp. 44–45.
4 Scott Sayre. Personal communication.
5 Marlene Chambers. "Is Anyone Out There? Audience and Communication." *Museum News* 62, 5 (June 1984): 47–54.
6 Smith. 2012, p. 45, note 12.
7 Judy Rand. "The 227-Mile Museum, or, Why We Need a Visitors' Bill of Rights." *Curator: The Museum Journal* 44, 1 (January 2001): 7–14.
8 AAMC 2015 Annual Conference and Meeting Itinerary. https://c.ymcdn.com/sites/artcurators.site-ym.com/resource/resmgr/2015_Conference/conference_itin erary_2015_fo.pdf Accessed July 25, 2015.

Part Two

Case Studies

In the chapters ahead, we present detailed case studies that bring to life the ideas and images exemplified by the museums we studied. The cases describe approaches crafted by museum professionals in the United States and abroad to create more visitor-centered museums. Our selection of museums is suggestive rather than exhaustive.

Highlighting the notion that no one size fits all, in our research we have seen an array of visitor-centered approaches and organizational changes to facilitate that transition. In the cases below, we share examples of this variation. We also see elements common to most museums in our study—elements integral to the very definition of visitor-centeredness.

As discussed, these changes are complex, including rewards, challenges, and repercussions. Usually, the organizational changes came about as a result of a commitment to a new or reinvigorated mission. What stands out is that all of the museums in this study share a commitment to prioritizing audience on an equal footing with collections and devote resources to meeting that goal.

It should be noted that many of the museums we studied were not in tourist destination cities. This proves to be a mixed blessing. On the one hand, they cannot rely on a steady stream of tourists and must find ways to encourage return visitation. Meeting their publics "where they are" is crucial to their survival. On the other hand, it gives these museums a freedom to experiment that their counterparts in major art world centers might not have.

Table P2.1 Six Elements Common to Visitor-Centered Museums

1. Formative audience research
2. Varied forms of integrated gallery interpretation
3. Community connection
4. A visitor-centered mission
5. Strong leadership (in service of that mission)
6. New forms of teamwork

A Visitor-Centered Continuum

As we conducted our field research, we began to see a visitor-centered continuum emerge. On the one hand, many colleagues had nominated City Museum—a haptic playground that is a delight to discover but a museum in name only—as a visitor-focused institution. On the other hand, many nominations fell into the normative, collection-based standard of museum practice. These were institutions that took the "collect-preserve-display" aspects of their mission rigorously to heart, yet wanted to match it with a new generosity toward the wider public. Finally, there were museums for whom the question of what a museum is and does—its very function in the culture today—came to the fore. These institutions were committed to an active critique of their own practice and that of their peers, critiques which sometimes took the form of irreverent reinvention, performance or satire. The spectrum of approaches is expressed in the continuum shown in Table P2.2.

The continuum begins and ends with institutions that are not strictly speaking collection based. In between these two antipodes, we progress from a twelve-story coal-washing plant that engulfs the visitor (the Ruhr Museum) into more normally scaled exhibitry with immersive components (the Minnesota History Center), and from there to an assortment of art and multidisciplinary museums intent on finding ways of making their collections relevant to the public. The final museums, including the collection-free MCA Denver, apply contemporary theory and performance (i.e., social practice) to connect with visitors. We'll treat each in its own time.

For historical perspective, we start in the middle of the continuum, at the Denver Art Museum. While the remaining cases will follow the order of the continuum, we make an exception in this instance, in order to begin at the beginning with this visitor-centered pioneer.

Table P2.2 An Approach to Organizing the Museums Treated in This Book

VISITOR-CENTERED MUSEUMS: A CONTINUUM OF APPROACHES

City Museum	Ruhr Museum	Minnesota History Ctr	Detroit Institute of Arts Kelvingrove Gallery	Denver Art Museum Columbus Art Museum Oakland Museum of CA	Van Abbe Museum	MCA Denver
PHYSICAL	IMMERSIVE	EMOTIVE	COGNITIVE +	CO-CREATIVE	META-COGNITIVE	

I Charting History

Moving forward by looking back, we start with the Denver Art Museum (DAM) and a historical overview. A leader in the field, DAM committed early on to a visitor-centered mission and pioneered the inclusion of audience research in exhibition design. In fact, as far back as the 1980s, Patterson Williams and Marlene Chambers, then directors of education and publications respectively, advocated for the inclusion of audience expertise as an essential part of the exhibition development process. Because of this foresight, DAM has a rich variety of interpretive resources integrated in its galleries. We see different types of didactics, poetic narratives, and hands-on creative activities. These resources are provided just in time, right in the gallery, and with comfortable seating available. The range of approaches matches a variety of learning styles and reasons for visiting.

Reflecting a need for different types of expertise, these rich visitor environments were created by new kinds of teams. This brought both challenge and opportunity for staff as curators, educators, and exhibition designers worked together in new ways. Finally, at DAM, visitor-centered change came with a director who had education high on his agenda and was not afraid to make needed institutional adjustments.

At DAM we see examples of all six elements common to most visitor-centered museums. In addition, we find a unique and historical perspective on creating change.

4 Denver Art Museum

Building a Sustainable Visitor-Centered Practice

Among all the museums we studied, Denver has the most longstanding tradition of visitor-centered practice. Taking a walk through its galleries provides the museum professional with two very different historical collections. The first, obvious to any visitor, comprises the artworks: Asian, American Indian, European, Western, Contemporary. The second is a living history of museum practice: the DAM provides a representative sampling of interpretive methods stretching back almost thirty years. As you move from the fortress-like North Building, designed by Gio Ponti and James Sudler in 1971, to the new, explosive silver shards of Daniel Libeskind's Hamilton Building—which opened in 2006—you can detect the traces of three generations of museum educators who first battled, then negotiated, and finally have come to partner with curators and exhibition designers in the creation of the DAM experience as we know it today.

There was a time in Denver, long ago, when even a seemingly innocuous chair became a bone of contention. Some of this timeworn furniture still exists, flanking small sidetables carrying catalogs in the Asian galleries. Hard to believe, but they are like markers on a battlefield documenting the tumultuous struggles of a previous generation. "When I showed up, the idea of putting a chair, a table, and a catalog in an exhibition was still considered radical," recalls Melora McDermott-Lewis, current DAM Director of Education. She joined the Denver team in 1986. Her predecessor and mentor, Patterson Williams, is old enough to be more outspoken, even outraged:

> The idea that you would change what labels had been was just excruciating—that you would add a chair to a gallery. There were one hundred seemingly rational reasons, the primary one of which was that it would block the line of view. Give me a break!

Notably, thirty years later, these simple first steps have still not yet been universally adopted in art museums.

In Denver, as in many other art museums, curators and educators once saw themselves as opposing teams in a zero-sum game. In many ways, museums of the 1980s still mirrored the academic division whereby serious scholarship

Figure 4.1 Denver Art Museum: seating in the Asian Art galleries.

was handled by men and junior education was given over to women and confined to school groups. The idea that these same educators might meddle in the serious business of gallery design was beyond the pale.

But as early as 1984, Williams and her colleague Marlene Chambers, Denver's Director of Publications, laid out the case for visitor-centered practice in a series of seminal articles that remain relevant to this day:

> Though they will admit that an introductory course in art appreciation may not be part of everyone's educational background, most art museum professionals discount this statistical reality in a way that diffuses its practical impact on their performance . . . First, we must find a way to analyze our audience's needs and interests. This can be done through surveys, informal interviews, and focus groups.[1]

Next, with such information and the visitor understanding that comes with it, museum practitioners can develop interpretive aids that speak to the layperson. And then, lest anyone think they're smart enough to get it right the first time . . .

> We must set up economical evaluation techniques to pinpoint our successes and failures. We must learn to pretest our label and brochure

texts, as well as to test their final effectiveness. We must be able and willing to improve them by revision.

We do not need to reinvent the wheel . . . [but] we must be prepared to give up some of our comfortable habits.

In 1982, Williams, for her part, had already laid out an overview of "Object-Oriented Learning in Art Museums" and would soon propose a comprehensive manifesto: "An Agenda for Reform":

Only by developing experts in audiences and in the ways that audiences learn and perceive, and by putting them in key leadership positions, can museums build a sufficient focus on the visitor's experience with art objects into annual budgets, long- and short-range planning, and the museum's staff structure.[2]

Clearly cognizant of the organizational hierarchies that put her at a disadvantage in her visitor advocacy, she wrote:

If we take one education expert and put that person on a committee with five or ten people without such expertise, that education expert will not succeed, no matter how strong he or she is as an individual . . . the traditional staff hierarchy in museums is an expression of values that place collecting activities and their staff experts in dominant roles and audience activities and their staff experts in subordinate roles. Changing such traditional power structures can be painful for all concerned.

She pointed out a power imbalance that many visitor advocates still encounter: "Usually [educators] are in junior positions from which they are powerless to do anything more than cajole others to consider the visitor's learning needs."

How often did we hear the teams we interviewed hark back to the patterns that had characterized their museums in the old days, before the advent of the new visitor-centered mission? Once communicating with visitors became a priority, inclusion of chairs, resources, and clear didactics was a natural response. Learning lounges were no longer a "nice to have" addition, "space permitting" once all the artwork was installed in the galleries. They were built into the exhibition layout from the start.

Williams' goal, seen in retrospect, was not so different from that of the curators: "to assist visitors to have peak experiences with art objects." The difference was that curators may not have had the data at hand to realize the degree of assistance visitors needed before they could connect with the art objects that were the very stuff of their own passion and livelihood. Among the raft of recommendations she offered were the following simple words:

We must encourage visitors to alter their behavior patterns on a museum visit—to slow down and concentrate on a small part of a collection rather than try to "see it all." Works of art are of a complex visual character . . . Comfortable seating can help.[3]

This helps us understand her exasperated guffaw as she looks back thirty years at the struggle to even get *chairs* into the gallery.

Of course seating alone is not enough—visitors insecure about looking at art may not even feel comfortable enough to take that seat. The Denver team began a long career producing *installed interpretives*: an evolving array of brochures, games, journals, videos, and analog and digital activities designed to support visitors in developing a deeper relationship with the artworks in the galleries. First came a multi-year action research project underwritten by the Getty Grant Program and the National Endowment for the Arts: the Denver Art Museum Interpretation Project (1988–1990). Interviewing visitors about their needs uncovered common behaviors and approaches to understanding. Museum staff targeted two groups of frequent visitors: "art novices" and "advanced amateurs." Both constituencies were predisposed to visit the museum, and both were susceptible to being led into deeper engagement with the art. The goal Williams, Chambers, and their colleagues set for themselves was to "help novices become more expert in, and more rewarded by, their encounters with works of art." Throughout the Ponti building, small seating pods popped up, accompanied by art books and more interactive ways of engaging visitors with the art: puzzles pegged at various levels of visual sophistication, comparison boards on which visitors were invited to arrange facsimiles of artworks in a fan-like spectrum of styles, "human connection cards" designed to make the artists as real to the visitors as they were to the curators, and journals inviting viewers to write themselves into a landscape painting on the wall before them.

In 1997 the museum opened a "Discovery Library" at the heart of its European paintings collection with all the burnished production values of a gentleman's curiosity cabinet: walls lined with bookcases filled with art books and objects; comfortable sofas and chairs; Renaissance paintings on one wall, an Egyptian mummy on another; cabinets with drawers that visitors were invited to pull open and examine, revealing fine prints or painted miniatures under glazing; and a costume closet for kids. It was designed as a deluxe discovery space for museum visitors of all ages—a taste of the elite world of those who had traditionally collected fine art. The colonialist and class message may feel a bit dated, but the gallery is still quite popular today.

Continuing through the DAM is like charting the forward progress of this gallery-based education in looking at art. "Okay, table with book in there. We sort of had our video nooks, then we had discovery libraries, then we integrated making," says McDermott-Lewis. "I would say, starting from the Eighties, we started with visitors' experiences and evolved what we want to do from what we heard from visitors." Each of the activities was treated as an experiment: informed by a hypothesis, it was then tested and evaluated. Experiment—Evaluate—Iterate: These have been the watchwords of

Figure 4.2a–b Denver Art Museum: Two views of the Discovery Library.

Denver's staff. Evaluations were sometimes Big-E and summative—that is, funded by major grants and contracted out to national consulting firms, yielding fully documented, formal reports—but more often small-e and formative: just-in-time gallery interviews in which staff conducted "structured conversations" with a small sampling of visitors to get feedback on activity mockups or label language. By frequent recourse to small-e evaluation, DAM staff could get immediate feedback on a mock-up or prototype, before proceeding to a more advanced and costly stage of design and production. Through publishing the results of these variously scaled tests, the DAM became a role model for the field.

Lewis Sharp, who arrived as director at the DAM from a curatorial post at New York's Metropolitan Museum of Art in 1989, was known first and foremost as a collections-and-building director, but his successor Christoph Heinrich will tell you, "Lewis really put education on top of his agenda. He saw that this was a way to become relevant." Sharp had clearly read Williams' manifesto and took her points to heart. He promoted her to the newly created position of Deputy Director for Education and instituted a new process for developing exhibitions: each curator would work in concert with a "master teacher" dedicated to his or her area. Together they would wed collection expertise with visitor research, and gradually come to know and appreciate each other's concerns. In this way they could more successfully collaborate with the museum's exhibition designers to develop galleries optimized for visitor experience. The transition was not always painless. McDermott-Lewis recalls: "I remember a time when we had a team process that was like sixteen pages long. You know: the educator gets to approve this on the third Thursday if the curator . . ." Gradually, over time, bridges of trust were built, paving the way to collaborative relationships that did not need to be legislated.

When the Hamilton Building was completed in 2006, the sharp, angular Daniel Libeskind design had many critics. It seemed to offer more challenges than affordances to the hanging of paintings, which after all do still typically come in flat, two-dimensional shapes intended for vertical—not sloping—walls. But if there were ever an art museum staff capable of making lemonade out of this problematic structure, it was the DAM's. After all, they had been performing research for over twenty years on ways of connecting visitors with their collections, and had devised myriad approaches that could be deployed in all those awkward, hard-to-hang spaces adjacent to the main galleries. The educators were not simply allocated the leftovers—the awkward, curatorially unusable spaces; the Hamilton wing opened with plentiful comfortable seating of every variety throughout the main galleries, as well as books, family games, reference materials, journals, and more "human connection cards"—now artfully designed laminated tri-fold brochures that visitors were invited to borrow, peruse, and return after use.[4]

The exhibition designers have risen to the challenge of making galleries that are both pristine spaces for viewing the artworks and context-rich

Figure 4.3a–b Denver Art Museum: Laminated "human connection cards" in the galleries.

Figure 4.4 Denver Art Museum Contemporary Galleries: facing a portrait wall, comfortable seating and a coffee table on which a creative challenge is placed: "Write a biography in six words."

environments offering interpretive paths and activities for non-specialist viewers. Reconciling these demands is not trivial, but has become a guiding principle of each reinstallation because curators now work side-by-side with subject-focused educators and designers specifically to serve audience needs.

Take, for example, the galleries dedicated to the art of the American West. Slipped unobtrusively into pockets on the wall at child height, Bingo cards with sliding windows provide treasure hunt clues to the artworks on view nearby. When the building opened, iPods with headphones were paired with leather-bound journals by the couches and chairs, facing key works of art. Each journal sported a different prompt on its cover: an invitation to visitors to sit down, tune into the art, use their chosen soundtrack as an aid to deepening their concentration, and then comment or compose. They were free to either take their writing home with them or leave it in the leather binder for others to read. Educators troll periodically through the galleries to check the journals and prune them as one would a garden, leaving perhaps the brightest blooms in the binders as well as comments reflecting a variety of approaches and ages so both kids and adults feel welcome to comment.

A bit further away, a maker space with drawing supplies and rubber stamps becomes a hub of activity as visitors make postcards to send to friends, take

Figure 4.5 Denver Art Museum: treasure hunt Bingo cards placed at child height.

away—or leave for public posting. The feeling remains one of comfortable, quiet, creative industry—of a museum inviting the participation of its community.

In the galleries devoted to African art, meanwhile, children sit in a hidden nook at floor level watching video of a tribal dance, while laminated color Human Connection brochures are once again available in pockets near the artworks they treat. Here, too, a maker space is near at hand. One of the lessons the DAM staff has learned is that adults—especially older ones—don't expect to engage in creative activities. Museum manners, after all, scrupulously train us not to touch anything in an art museum. So the museum staff has set themselves the task of re-educating their visitors as to what is permissible in their galleries. (See Appendix B: *Lessons Learned: Adult Gallery Activities at the Denver Art Museum.*)

Now, the experiments that began in the 1980s, matured in the 1990s, and came to abundant fruition with the 2006 opening of the Hamilton Building are circling back into the original Ponti galleries (dubbed the North Building and ripe for a remodel). The first gallery to get the new treatment was devoted to the DAM's superb American Indian collection—coincidentally the purview of the DAM's Chief Curator, Nancy Blomberg. Working together with Master Teacher Heather Nielsen and designers KPC and Elroy Quenroe,

Figure 4.6 Denver Art Museum: visitors in a maker space adjacent to the galleries.

the exhibition development team had very specific experience and interpretive objectives, including liberating the objects from the traditional ethnographic approach seen in so many museums around the world.

The majority of works are presented without vitrines on platforms that keep the objects safely out of arm's reach. The emphasis is no longer on viewing them as tribal artifacts from dead cultures, but rather as artworks made by creative individuals in traditions that live on today. Although the names of nineteenth-century makers may be unknown to us, contemporary Indian artists are interviewed and presented in videos as part of a living tradition. These videos and multimedia interactives are installed directly in the galleries, amid the artworks.

Blomberg: We felt they had to be located in key places, because we were presenting core ideas in these; and that people would then be drawn to them, listen to them, interact, whatever, and then take those and bounce off the rest of the gallery. And it *was* a discussion that we didn't want them to distract from the artwork.

And you know, I'm probably a little conservative in that point of view, and I'm going, 'Uh, how prominent, how big are the screens going to be?' I liked the concept, but was very concerned that it would not distract, but that it had to complement. And we worked very hard with the designers to make them so that they're not distracting . . . They will pull you in; they're compelling, you want to see them. But then you take whatever concept we're presenting and go bounce off all the platforms.

Neilsen: I mean, I think we have a history at this institution, of always having tried to push that interpretation, you know, could happen near objects. And of course, there's a lot of conversation involved in that. And every curator-educator team, I think, has approached that always very differently. But I would agree with Nancy. I mean, it never was even a discussion, whether or not all interpretation would be in one corner and all artwork would be someplace else.

DAM creative teams have also realized that different gallery configurations support different activities and needs. While the interpretive resources are braided through the collection galleries, The Bead Studio, a maker space, lies just beyond them, still within view. It is an example of DAM's increasing focus on moving beyond the didactic to foster visitors' own creative engagement—always informed by the objects on view. In one spot, visitors are invited to sit at a table and pursue the deceptively simple act of setting colored marbles into a matrix that somewhat resembles a Chinese checkerboard. The activity was developed by master educator Neilsen after she went into the field and "did her ethnography"—interviewing Indian bead artists about their work. "What is it about being an artist?" she asked. "Well, you need patience. You know, it's about how color goes together. It's about [how] we come together in bead circles." So now families come and sit together at this table and bead together. In the words of one mother who described her experience in the galleries:

> We've actually been to these bead tables, Grandpa, me and my four-year-old son. Those two will sit right next to each other at the same time, do their own thing and help each other. I love that it transcends age levels.[5]

The DAM has repeated this creative impulse in their recent Thread Studio, and taken it further by opening a live studio space on the ground floor that can be adapted to reflect the major temporary exhibition of the season. In the "Marvelous Mud" summer of 2011, eight different shows focused on ceramic art. On the ground floor, a "Mud Studio" welcomed visitors as local artists demonstrated their expertise and visitors got to try their hand. A year later, to coincide with an Yves Saint-Laurent show, the space was transformed into a "Fashion Studio" in which local designers rotated through, showing visitors how to drape and cut fabric or draw from the model. The space has subsequently been transformed into an interactive paint, sculpture, and jewelry studio, depending on the content of the highlighted exhibition.

On Reflection

The surprising and enlivening lesson that Denver has learned after twenty-plus years of experimenting, evaluating, and iterating is that in the final analysis, listening to visitors is empowering, not constraining. Quite simply, more data leads to better decisions. Staff has come to see trying something new in the gallery as an opportunity for a breath of fresh air that allows not just the visitor, but the organization itself, to learn—as opposed to vetoing installed interpretives, which has often been the reflex response in more traditional art museums. In the words of Melora McDermott-Lewis:

> I think one of the things that's been striking to me over twenty to twenty-five years is that when we get something tangible into the gallery, it's like the boogie man disappears . . . When [curators] hear from real visitors, versus from educators talking about real visitors, interesting things happen.

She describes how, at a visitor panel, curators had a direct conduit to their audience and got more involved than anyone else. As Chief Curator Blomberg says: "You have to know your audience. Who are you creating this exhibit for? We're not doing it for us." She describes the difficult (and unprecedented) decision she made to reprint all the labels in the American Indian galleries once they got the results of the summative evaluation:

Blomberg:　Yes, visitor feedback said they're too small. And this is always a challenge, you know? Because you don't, again, want the labels to take away from the objects; and in many instances, they might be half the size of an object. Visitors told us: "No. We can't read them." We literally went back and doubled the size and reprinted every label. . . . Three months after the exhibit went in, we printed all new labels, twice the size. Literally, 700 new labels. And people can now read them.

The experience of reprinting labels once again reinforces the notion that we all benefit from having access to data. This is true for educators, designers, and curators alike. Furthermore, data-driven research shows us that information fosters shared agency and collaboration. Rather than withhold information or restrict it to educators alone, we should expand our reach to include all colleagues who might value this knowledge. In most other museums, the curators haven't asked for—or been given—the information and audience contact necessary to make truly visitor-centered decisions.

Key Takeaways

1. Listening to visitors is empowering. More data leads to better decisions for everyone.
2. At DAM, curators collaborate with subject area "master teachers" to plan exhibitions and interpretive strategies together. New ways of working generate new ideas as well as staff growth.
3. Plentiful gallery seating is a first step in meeting visitor needs. Installed interpretives, both analog and digital, can go the extra mile. DAM's discovery libraries, creative studios, and learning lounges unite comfortable seating with art-related activities right in the galleries. Multiple approaches are vital.
4. While a visitor-centered approach does not come naturally to art museums, it can come to life with a clearly articulated, visitor-centered mission and the support of leadership.

Notes

1 Marlene Chambers. "Is Anyone Out There? Audience and Communication." *Museum News* 62, 5 (June 1984): 47.
2 Patterson Williams. "Educational Excellence in Art Museums: An Agenda for Reform." *Journal of Aesthetic Education* 19, 2 (Summer 1985): 105–123.
3 Patterson Williams. "Object-Oriented Learning in Art Museums." *Roundtable Reports* 7, 2 (1982): 12–15. Williams' comment raises questions about admission fees in museums: paying per admission puts pressure on visitors to see all they can.
4 The seating, by the way, is not to be taken for granted. Even when we find seating, it is not necessarily comfortable. The flat wooden bench is a frequent art museum standard and presents a challenge to older visitors who may have difficulty rising from it. It's essential to consider what constitutes comfortable gallery seating.
5 Daryl Fischer. "Denver Art Museum IMLS Project Front-End Visitor Panel Debriefing Meeting Report." Grand Haven: Musynergy, 2012, p. 3.

II Engaging through Audience Immersion

From Denver's pioneering achievements, we move our discussion to the left end of the continuum, to three immersive environments, where we follow the rest of the cases in sequence. City Museum, Ruhr Museum, and the Minnesota Historical Society's History Center (MNHS) are three immersive museums that flood their visitors with sensations, albeit in very different ways.[1] Two are history-based, and one, City, is . . . well, hardly a museum at all. In all three places, emotional engagement—felt experience—is primary.

While these museums serve public interests, they also expand our notions of the museum experience itself. This is most apparent at City, which in some ways is more like an amusement park than a traditional museum.

Of the three, Ruhr—with its anchor of a specific collection and some conventional displays—might have the most traditional approach, yet through imaginative design, it sucks us into its distinctly non-traditional industrial shell. While the other two may use objects, they don't rely on them. In fact, at City Museum, where play and adventure are paramount, any collections, if present, are in the background. At MNHS, stories, not objects, drive the exhibits.

These three museums are very different from each other and from others in this study. As founder-driven museums, City and Ruhr have been shaped by unique and idiosyncratic leaders. This type of founder vision is not only hard to emulate, but, with its self-inspired purpose, may not always conform to the criteria we have stated for visitor-centeredness. For instance, these two museums differ from others we have studied in their de-emphasis on traditional types of visitor research and forms of teamwork. In fact, at City Museum or Ruhr, while teams were necessary, they mainly served to execute the bidding of a visionary leader, not to work together to fulfill a shared visitor-centered goal. This might be true of their audience research as well: if present, it may have been focused on fulfilling a leader's particular goals.

On the other hand, MNHS fully illustrates all six visitor-centered elements we have outlined: the importance of audience research, mission, community, teamwork, leadership, and varied interpretive modes. Minnesota History Center's generative process is team-based and interdisciplinary and relies heavily on visitor research. The teams' mission is to emotionally engage specific target audiences through each exhibition, in service to the larger purpose of reaching a diverse public.

Through their focus on play, immersive scenography, and emotional engagement, all three museums, while different in ways we shall describe, enrich our notion of what it means to be visitor-centered. Critically, all three share the goal of quickly wowing the visitor with an emotional connection. As a valuable reminder of how important felt experience really is, these museums challenge us to consider what we deem museum-worthy content.

Note

1 The History Center uses the abbreviation of its parent organization.

5   City Museum
The Power of Play

At City Museum, play is the way to connect to community. In other words, at any age, it's okay just to play. The museum focuses on kids but offers experiences for visitors of all ages and abilities. It is premised on the idea that each person can perform—and find something to delight in—at his or her own level. The staff oversees, manages risk, and tries to make sure that all visitors feel safe and have a good time.

•

St. Louis's City Museum is arguably more of a multi-story indoor and outdoor playground than a museum—yet it bears the name and has served as inspiration for enough museum professionals to merit consideration here. Founded in 1997 in an abandoned shoe factory near St. Louis's downtown, its presence and popularity have played a role in the revival of that neighborhood. City Museum is a hive of activity, spilling out into the surrounding streets above and below: fire trucks and planes have been seized and welded into its Monster playground armature, a yellow school bus juts from its brow, and a Ferris wheel crowns its thirteenth-story roof. The whole is animated by the manic activity of hundreds of kids, crawling like ants through open steel mesh conduits that lift them through the air in defiance of gravity, arcing from one destination to another, holding them in an airborne matrix above the city block, amid buildings left over from St. Louis's distant and defunct manufacturing past.

Everywhere there is movement, indoors and out, through a hundred hidden passages and downward spirals; if venturing into the unknown to discover new sights and sensations is the essence of adventure, then City Museum is an adventurer's paradise.

Physical exertion is part of the deal—as is temporary disorientation. Changing your posture equals altering your perspective. It is the path to exuberance and revelation. Get on your belly and slither through tubes and cracks and holes in a Gaudí-esque concrete garden. Pull yourself up through mid-air. As one child said to another: "It's so cool. If you can fit there, you

Figure 5.1 City Museum: children in aerial tubes above "Monster" playground.

Figure 5.2 City Museum: first floor grotto, reached via a ten-story slide.

can *go* there." The place is designed to provoke a sense of curiosity, wonder, and discovery at every step of the way.

"There's a moment when you walk into the caves, through that tunnel," says Director Rick Erwin III. "It's dark, it's dark, and all of a sudden you're at The Crystal and you look up . . . and when kids come in for the first time you just hear—there's no sound or there's just a big scream. And you know it's working for them."

City was the creation of a charismatic anarchist, a sculptor named Bob Cassilly who believed that art has a public vocation and should be synonymous with fun, discovery, and community empowerment. He built immersive interactive adventure playgrounds characterized by meticulous craftsmanship—tiling, welding, and design—that have become pilgrimage environments for people of all ages who return to them again and again.

Senior citizens who know the place often show up just to feel part of a lively community and watch the younger families and kids excitedly tearing around. If you're a parent, don't expect to bring your kids and then go sit on a bench to tranquilly read your iPad. In his day, Cassilly would have confiscated it, seeing it as symptomatic of a parent unwilling to join their child on a discovery adventure. Sometimes, adults visiting for the first time ask if they have to pay for themselves as well; they assume the place is just for kids—but they are sorely mistaken. "There's nothing better than when kids clap for an adult who just did something," says Erwin. City Museum is designed as a place where everybody can let go together and bond in the sheer excitement of a moment in which adults rediscover the inner child they forgot.

"I always see adults who go, 'Oh my God! I can't believe I did this!'" says Stephanie Van Drasek, who has been working at the museum since 1999. "I'm like: 'You're going to go home, and you're going to have muscles you forgot you had tomorrow, you know?' You can reconnect with yourself—not just artistically, but physically, through a visit here." City Museum functions on the premise that mind and body are not separate. There's nothing academic about it; it's just about making. This is a museum entirely based in Maker Culture.

Yes, there are some collections: one of terra cotta architectural fragments salvaged from great buildings of old St. Louis before they were torn down, another of dolls and other somewhat moth-eaten curiosities, not to mention a somewhat lugubrious aquarium of sorts. And yes, at its inception, Cassilly and his then-wife Gail, the co-founder, incorporated City as a non-profit and briefly flirted with museum accreditation. They had a board of trustees and development and education directors, but that ended badly. All of these forces of bureaucratization clashed with the antic spirit of Bob Cassilly. "He just wanted to be able to come in and tear apart and build," says Von Drasek, and he was not about to ask anyone for permission first. After a very public showdown on the St. Louis courthouse steps, a messy divorce, and the resignation of the board, Cassilly recruited a silent partner and turned City Museum into a for-profit corporation that gave him the power to do exactly what he wanted, when he wanted.

"He didn't want a Museum," says Von Drasek, motioning to the hive of activity around her. "He wanted *this* . . . He didn't set out to create a museum; he just set out to build something neat and—okay, people will come. So we went about it kind of backwards, in that way." Director Erwin picks up: "Bob was this huge figure. He was just charismatic and really knowledgeable—just extremely intelligent. He was like a parent to us. Like, if Bob's around, nothing's going to happen to you. I mean, he's the strongest man I ever met. When he was in the building, everything changed. He had full energy, people fed off of him." City Museum had all the benefits and liabilities of a charismatic founder-driven institution.

Cassilly often operated with utter conviction: "Sometimes, the only way to end a debate or discussion around here was 'Bob said *no*,'" says Tracey La Riccia, who runs field trips and sleep-overs for the school groups and scout troops who come to the museum—and don't get much sleep. "Or the way to get something done, no matter what it was: 'Bob wants it done.'" adds Von Drasek. "That's why there's a bus hanging off the roof."

Over the years, even city officials and building inspectors bowed to the inexorable force of Bob Cassilly. They came to understand that his "museum" was one of the prime draws helping to re-animate what had been a dying urban core and green-lighted even the most unlikely projects. "After a while, they would kind of look the other way and say: 'All right, he knows what he's doing. He'll get it taken care of.'"

Staff consists of a bare bones management team of four, plus Bob's gang of fellow artist-craftsmen, a maintenance crew, and a rotating crew of 75–125 young and enthusiastic floor staff who function like camp counselors helping to ensure the safety and good times of the visitors.

Discovery, tech, and science museums may try to harness the boundless energy and curiosity of kids and tether them to learning goals, but Cassilly had no such curricular ambitions. He felt the life lessons kids needed to learn had less to do with academic subjects than with daring and risk-taking—having the courage to follow the fear/joy razor's edge of your own curiosity. He believed that where joy flowed, life provided its own guidance, and he valued self-directed wonder more than any book-learning.

That spirit worked for him for many years. It certainly propelled the team of artisan craftsmen who worked with him, keeping the museum in a perpetually evolving state of development. Cassilly's drive eventually led him to venture into a far more ambitious project: the transformation of a multi-acre site, a former Portland cement works across the river—which was where, working alone on a weekend in 2011, he rolled his bulldozer, beaned his unprotected head on the unforgiving steel cab roof, and hemorrhaged to death.

Predictably, along with the shock and mourning, a succession struggle ensued, with old team members coming out of the woodwork, each of them claiming to embody the True Spirit of Bob. "Everybody wanted to take over," says Erwin. "Everybody wanted to be Creative Director. And we just said 'No. There will be no Creative Director. If we're going to do it, we're going to do it as a collective.'" And so Bob's team was paid to stay in place. "I got to hire his entire crew that worked with him. Thirty years of knowledge of working with Bob. Because we wanted to make sure they all stayed together." The whole team has been directly imprinted—seared by his zeal, scalded by his temper, and inspired by his ceaseless urge to push the boundaries. They're Bob Cassilly's brain-and-brawn trust: his legacy lives on in their muscles and know-how.

Not surprisingly, Cassilly left a multitude of unfinished projects—enough to keep his team going for quite a while. They've also begun to venture into new ones (e.g., remodeling the gift shop) in a way they feel remains true to his spirit.

While City Museum was recommended by many museum colleagues as a particularly inspiring example of visitor-centeredness, if you ask Rick Erwin III about the kinds of focus groups, visitor panels, or evaluations that characterize many other museums studied in this book, he will scoff.

> Everything I learned in Arts Administration, I haven't used a single bit of it here. The first thing I think about when we start designing is how it makes my stomach feel. If I feel a little queasy here, and I feel a little bit scared, I know we're on the right track . . . Everything we build is what we think is fun and cool. It's great the customers have liked it. We do think about their safety. We hope we inspire them. We hope they get lost while they're here. We hope they hang out with their kids. . . . But we're not getting any maps, because I don't want to control how you see things.

There's no technology, either. Nothing that can break or needs constant maintenance. "We build stuff out of concrete and metal so we don't have to watch it as much."

While museums and libraries from as far afield as Scandinavia and Singapore make pilgrimages to St. Louis to study City Museum and try to understand its secret sauce, there's no org chart, no board, and no mission statement. Except perhaps one Cassilly favored, sourced from *Moby Dick*.

"We seek the white whale."

Key Takeaways

1. Fun and physical engagement are fulfilling in their own right.
2. Play welcomes all ages—delighting the young, while sometimes challenging the old. Play offers another way to connect to community.
3. Play turns visitors into participants: it creates an emotional connection that promotes loyalty to the institution. Fans share their love of the institution through social media and word of mouth—and by coming back again and again.
4. With support, it's okay to ask people to stretch beyond their comfort zone.

6 Ruhr Museum
Connecting through Adaptive
Reuse and Design

At Ruhr, a different kind of immersive site, we see community connection in various ways. Here, adaptive reuse of a huge industrial structure proved more powerful than building from scratch. By remaking a once important but inaccessible site, homage is paid to local industrial history even as a new cultural space is made available for the public. The artful inclusion of objects drawn from the community's own memory honors the local people and connects them to their institution. Ruhr reminds us that humble objects and stories can offer emotional connections both local and universal.

•

What if you took the funky, antic playspace of the City Museum and flipped it into a high design experience zone for a multisensory exploration of human knowledge, seen through the lens of one spot on the planet? Perhaps not surprisingly, you would have landed at the Ruhr Museum in Essen, Germany.

Both City and Ruhr museums are immersive. Both are crafted from abandoned industrial sites that in other circumstances might have been slated for the wrecking ball. Both engage your body and senses on an experiential trip; one drops you down from the roof on a ten-story spiral slide while the other sucks you up seven stories to begin your journey. However, the similarities, while remarkable, are not as instructive as the differences. For while the City Museum tickles your curiosity and stretches your limits through a promise of perpetual play, the Ruhr Museum plunges you into bunkers of memory redolent of times past.

The site itself is a spectacular framework within which the museum is housed. It was built between 1929 and 1932 to connect with a mine head that drew rock churned up from 1000 meters deep. An International Style modernist factory envelope writ on a grand scale, with skin of brown bricks and glass, its curtain walls hide what was once a vast, multi-story, self-contained machine: a coal-washing plant. Less than a century ago, this was the largest and most efficient coalmine in the world.[1] In 2001, it was declared a UNESCO World Heritage Site, a relic from Europe's industrial age.

Figure 6.1 Ruhr Museum: exterior view.

The original building had no entrance per se: some eighty workers climbed into the huge machine via a ladder in its side wall. Rem Koolhaas/OMA, charged with the adaptive reuse plan, saw an opportunity: they inserted a dramatic induction tube, a glazed double escalator rising seven stories from the ground in a 190-foot-long neon orange ribbon. You are metaphorically processed into this factory/museum via conveyor belt—a physical movement that mirrors the transition from the industrial age to today's knowledge and experience economy.

Crossing the threshold at the 24-Meter Level, you enter a new zone: an environment that mixes old industrial forms with clean modern graphics and museum amenities we have come to expect, such as information desks and a café. You don't linger long, for you have risen this high only to descend like a pinball down an interior orange staircase, not a spiral but a square, looking like nothing so much as molten steel being channeled lower and lower into the earth, into layers of memory—personal, collective, cultural, and geologic.

The Ruhr Museum is born of the confluence of many fields: geology, pale-ontology, archaeology, natural history, and biology. It includes collections sourced in medieval times, in the industrial era, and even in the everyday lives of the residents of the Ruhr Valley today. It is a transplant from a pre-existing regional museum once housed in the city's center.

Figure 6.2 Ruhr Museum: ascending the seven-story ribbon of escalator.

Just as City Museum was the work of many hands but the vision of only one, Bob Cassilly, so too Ruhr has been forged by many specialists brought together under the unifying leadership of one man, Ulrich Borsdorf. It was Borsdorf's vision to create this three-tiered plunge into the imagined past and to house it in this setting. "I learned to make exhibits in industrial ruins," he says. "And those ruins were saved from destruction by making exhibits in them—because people loved those exhibits so much that nobody could imagine their destruction anymore."

Borsdorf points out the pent-up public curiosity about what took place behind these walls—the machinery that had defined the region's economy, its workforce's principal employment, and its polluted air and water for many generations. "Nobody had been allowed to enter these objects. So these were hidden spaces. And although it was the experienced space of thousands of workers, their families and the other public was not allowed to see them."

Koolhaas, too, had insisted that rather than build a separate museum on the mine site, the original industrial structures must be used to preserve maximum impact. The power of spectacle is not to be underrated: industrial reuse provides an immersive experience and honors the local community by highlighting its history.

It was one thing to have a spectacular container, but it still remained to populate it, and to determine how exactly its contents would be presented. That was where Borsdorf brought together his team, each specializing in a particular academic discipline, and assigned them to work together in new teams, each producing a *DenkSchrift*: a detailed illustrated thinkpiece envisioning an aspect of the new museum's themes and the objects that would bring them to life. The process was lengthy; three years of research led to a complete briefing book. "And then we printed it and said 'What bullshit we have produced!'" exclaims Borsdorf. "And re-discussed the whole concept for another year. And then we went back to the first idea."

It was a radical departure, one based on memory theory: a history museum that starts in the living memory of its visitors, and then leapfrogs backwards, only to end by zooming forward to the present. Begin not with historic treasures but with people as they are today, with the region in all its diversity, reborn in the post-industrial, multi-ethnic palette of contemporary Europe.

Once Borsdorf and his team had confirmed their knowledge model—and the objects and arguments that would flow from it—they brought in the exhibition designers, organizing a competition between six leading European firms. The bidders openly presented their proposals before a multi-disciplinary selection panel during a grueling two-day convening. Everybody got to hear everyone else. And when the winning firm was selected—H. G. Merz

Figure 6.3 Ruhr Museum: descending into the exhibits guided by a tablet.

from Stuttgart—they were given a great deal of latitude to develop and propose a design. "It is very rare that a professor of paleontology knows or can
decide or judge on the presentation," admonishes Borsdorf. "How is the
object to be seen? From what side can you look at it? Is it high or low? How
is the light positioned to reveal all the crucial information?"

In this model, content specialists select the objects and prepare the highly
detailed briefing books; exhibition architects are then charged with designing display and communication systems, with visitor experience first and
foremost in mind. For history museums, that model may be somewhat
standard—but at Ruhr, their intervention was virtuosic.

So what happens when we are processed down that square flume of a
staircase?

We move into the past by starting with the present. Stepping off the staircase at the 17-Meter Level, we discover pristine white walls set within the
dark, russet-colored steel interior: ribbons of backlit transparencies echo-
ing the external factory windows but full of variety, color, and life. They
depict life today in the Ruhr Region, home to fifty-three towns and cities
and more than eight million people. It is a population far more diverse than
the stereotypical, downtrodden "Ruhries" of old—depressed mineworkers
and their sickly, sun-deprived children. The luminous photos vividly portray
immigrants of every stripe and cultural tradition engaged in the acts of daily
living. Certain passions unite them—for example, football.[2] The trophies and
paraphernalia of the local teams are displayed in vitrines, tongue-in-cheek, as
religious relics. "You don't expect to see things about the Dortmund soccer
team in a museum," says Sandra Sorgenicht, director of Communications
and Marketing. "The Ruhries, they love it very much. For them it's very
important. It's part of their history—and it's unexpected here."

"At the first level, we catch them," says Sorgenicht. The photos are
complemented by inputs for the other senses as well: a smell machine—a
minimalist white box with a grid of buttons on it, each to trigger a scent;
a sound garden, its sampled sound-showers multiplied by the number of
people standing on dots on the floor; and a glass-paned herbarium mixing
and mating indigenous and non-native species. (Yet another metaphor for
intercourse among human populations where master race myths are now
obsolete.)

All of these "Phenomena"—visual, acoustic, olfactory, botanical—are
complemented by one of the rare instances of computer technology in the
entire museum: a data visualization zone presenting a set of compelling
graphics that powerfully convey "Ruhr by the Numbers." So there is something here for geeks, too. The museum is clearly differentiating itself from
the quaint and corny *Heimat* museums: Germany's many local heritage sites
which emphasize craft and folk life.

But what's really arresting is what happens when you move through the
air lock glass doors at the rear of the floor, which open onto a muted zone:
a sacred space of sorts.

Figure 6.4 Ruhr Museum: *The Present: Signs of the Times*. Entrance.

Before you stands an array of white bull-nosed pillars ascending from floor to ceiling, each one containing a glass case, aquarium-like, revealing an object, *a specimen*: a rock, a lung, a jar of water. And on each glass case, a word or phrase.

Atemlos. *Breathless*. Placed over an ambiguous piece of coiled black matter. Tissue in formaldehyde. Black lung.

Not a standard label, but a counterpoint. Already, from the moment of visual impact, a poetic point of view. Not didactic, but a feeling: out of breath. Terminal. Just a specimen now, but once in someone's body. A miner's. A local. Someone who spent his entire life working underground. Perhaps just below where we stand today.

Each of the exhibits in this silent zone is an object in similarly suspended animation. Condensors of memory, of meaning. We read their stories—in German or English—and contemplate the objects to which they refer: one per vitrine, isolated, preserved in a sort of incandescent limbo, offered up to our gaze and attention: a concentrate of the human experience specific to this site.

More often than not, the objects are humble. Design Aesthetics meet Storytelling, begetting Human Emotion . . . in concise and pristine form, pitched at a scale people can understand. Borsdorf, his curators, and H. G Merz have taken their aesthetic from contemporary art. Could it be that minimalism

 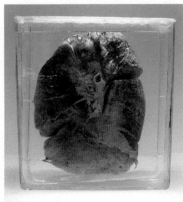

Figure 6.5 Ruhr Museum: *Signs of the Times*. First object in exhibit.

works better as a design language to showcase dramatically charged historical, zoological, and medieval specimens than as an art form in and of itself?

Consider this souvenir of a bourgeois childhood only recognized as sheltered in retrospect, two wars later, after double onslaughts of bombs and blood. Custom-crafted dollhouse furniture recovered amid the ruins of a broken country, mimicking the adult furnishings of a family's house and evoking an ease long lost. The legend on the glass reads: I didn't dare to touch it.

But not all the signs are of tragedy and war: "In China, I was Mister Hans." We know how the Germans pride themselves on their beer. A local brewmeister takes early retirement, but answers an ad in a trade publication for advice setting up a brewery in China. By 2004 he has helped set up fifteen of them. The Chinese find a way of honoring him by merging his name with their dynasty in a special brew. Four different breweries come out with tribute beers, all featuring his name. One has his portrait on the label. Such are the ties that bind us together across the world: affection, pride in an excellent product, savvy marketing, and love of beer—not to mention the effects it produces!

Fascinating and revealing. This is museum voice at its best. Episodes in the lives of individuals that open potent doors onto the life of a culture. Evocative, dramatic, meaningful.

Figure 6.6 Ruhr Museum: *Signs of the Times*. Exhibit of doll furniture.

Figure 6.7 Ruhr Museum: *Signs of the Times*. Exhibit of beer bottles with Chinese labels.

On the next level down, we continue our journey through this carefully crafted magic theater. The 12-Meter Level begins with the mastodon and the rhino.

Animals that once roamed here in the company of *homo neanderthalensis*— long before humans and their culture came to dominate and define the terrain. This is the level of *Gedachtnis*, the pre-industrial memory of the region.

This level did not exist in the original coal-washing plant: it was carved out from huge, concrete storage bunkers which then became square galleries with sloping, coal-blackened walls. Held up against these brute and scarred surfaces, swords from the time of Charlemagne, once forged to slay, now lie brittle and pitted, spotlit in the darkness. A far cry from the stuff on which conquests are built. Religious reliquaries: hand-tooled gold clasps, supports for sacred scriptures, receptacles for holy liniments—all are set against walls more reminiscent of an Anselm Kiefer painting of scarred earth and lead than of the glory of a heavenly chapel. We stand in post-industrial catacombs, now home to these object-refugees from the Middle Ages. Transplanted from one tomb to another, with no loss of effect. It seems that anything put in these brute timeworn spaces and lit with a pinspot will give you the shivers.

Figure 6.8 Ruhr Museum: 12-Meter Level (History).

Outside the bunkers, a succession of scenographies:

- Engravings of Renaissance towns, each once an independent city-state. Before each, a vitrine: archaeological finds and debris found while rebuilding after bombardments.
- Bones piled in cubbies, a black wall of birds arrayed in a grid. All stripped from their environment: these are specimen catalogue collections, displays of knowledge made corporeal. The taxonomic impulse vividly rendered—even without the names.

And in the midst of it all, this parade of animals.

Which makes the fall into mere History, at the lowest, 6-Meter Level, all the more disappointing. Here, after having been by turns moved and enthralled at the previous levels, we enter a standard history museum—presenting a superabundance of objects on a ninety-meter succession of metaphorical conveyors: platforms taking us from the birth of coal in mineral swamps through its discovery and instrumentalization in the Industrial Era, culminating in the larger-than-life figure of Alfred Krupp, coal and steel magnate—and wait, that's not all, rocketing forward from there through World War II, the Nazis, the Jewish lives liquidated—each a flickering star extinguished on a wall—and the few voices of resistance

Figure 6.9 Ruhr Museum: parade of native species on the 12-Meter Level.

Figure 6.10 Ruhr Museum: artifact and information "conveyors" at 6-Meter Level. Photo: Brigida González.

standing out against the monolithic wall of Nazi propaganda, while a felled American bomber propeller stands like a twisted cruciform sculpture nearby. The war over, the conveyor shoots forward: the Cold War, pollution, the closure of the mines, the rise of environmentalism. It's all too much in too little space. We were already tired, super-saturated. Now we turn numb.

As we have made our journey, the museum's presentation modes have evolved: from pristine contemporary media and minimalist object stories on the top levels to mysterious relics and animal taxonomies on the middle. Until now, the displays have successfully titrated information to meet our needs. However, at the lowest level, it is as if a whole new museum begins, one designed for visitors who are just arriving. Just as we reach a satisfying saturation point, the museum shifts into data overdrive.

What happened? Borsdorf confesses his misgivings:

> I was in deep doubt whether one can really show history in objects. But in history, you have two principles that you cannot abolish: the course of time . . . and you have to be more or less complete. Perhaps we should have been more courageous, and not had chronology.

He suggests that organizing by subject areas would have given them greater freedom to design with visitor experience in mind. "But for historians, this is very hard to realize. If we would have had more time, perhaps . . ."

By the end, we miss the elegance, the spareness, the clarity of those early Signs of the Times. We have been overwhelmed by collections. This is an important lesson: when collections are given priority over experience, experience suffers.

In the next chapter, we shall examine the Minnesota History Center, where through a very different process they have learned that if you emphasize serving the visitor, collections take a back seat.

Key Takeaways

1. Sensory-rich and immersive design primes visitors for deeper messages. Ruhr exhibits appeal to multiple senses. Never underestimate the power of immersive and experiential design.
2. Humble objects and succinct stories presented in a striking manner can be powerfully evocative.
3. Beware the pitfall of trying to fit in too many objects, graphics, or talking points.
4. Cognitive overload leads to fatigue and disengagement.

Notes

1 Christiane Borgelt and Regina Jost. *Zollverein World Heritage Site Essen*. Berlin: Stadtwandel Verlag, 2009, p. 10.
2 American soccer.

7   Minnesota History Center
Lessons from a Learning Team

Focused on engaging visitors from the get-go, at the Minnesota History Center we find another immersive museum whose leader is clear about his visitor-oriented mission and about how best to direct his team. Working at children's museums taught Dan Spock, the History Center's director, about the importance of play and the emotional resonance of stories as a vital means of connecting with visitors of all ages.

The museum's teams produce immersive experiences that plunge visitors into the visceral heart of a story. They hook visitors and then build on that original emotional connection. MNHS goes beyond play to make history personal.

The Minnesota Historical Society manages two collections: one of objects, the other of stories. For Spock and his teams, sharing stories and provoking experiences that give rise to meaningful conversations is more important than showcasing collection objects.

•

The Minnesota Historical Society (MNHS) runs more than twenty-five venues throughout the state, from house museums to old trading posts, forts, and factories, but its main administrative offices and collections center are situated in a modern building in St. Paul, near the State Capitol. There, in the Minnesota History Center, one might expect to find an emphasis on the jewels of their 250,000-object collection—but this is far from the case. Over two decades of practice, the History Center team has learned that "the process of creating an exhibition is independent from the process of collecting objects."

"I inherited a program that had already made the decision that this was going to be a museum for the general public, not for enthusiasts or aficionados," says Dan Spock, the History Center's museum director. From that clarity, a whole set of corollaries follows, of which the most important one is: "We're starting with people. We're starting with who this is for." "And we're always thinking about experience first," adds Kate Roberts, Senior Exhibit Developer.

At the History Center we are in conversation with a group—and a tight-knit one at that. A high performance team. Unlike City Museum or the Ruhr, where teams mainly served to execute the bidding of a visionary leader, the Minnesota History Center's generative process is team-based and interdisciplinary, born of the processes outlined in the 1988 Kellogg Foundation study that led to the book *Open Conversations.*

"We don't say 'curator' here," says Jennifer Sly, whose official title is Museum Education and Technology Specialist. However, people don't take much stock in titles at the MNHS. They are more interested in how each person contributes to the exhibition development process and its impact on visitor experience.

Core teams at the History Center comprise a project manager, a content expert, a three-dimensional designer, a graphic designer, and—in cases where there is a curriculum component—an educator. Later in the process, team members with media production, theatrical, and lighting experience may join in.

"I think that for me, there are the moments when I'm like 'Oh, I love this': when we've got a floor plan in front of us and we're at that phase in development where you've got all these different perspectives around the table and we're just putting stuff out there, you know? We're like, making stuff up. When it works right, it's this sort of energy and thrill of creating something." That's Kate Roberts again. Spock adds: "I always liken it to watching a Polaroid develop in front of your eyes. I love that moment when it suddenly starts to become real . . . and when it exceeds your expectations and you can think back to when you started and you realize it's better even than that, than the promise it held at the very beginning."

The reason it exceeds that promise is the synergy of the team process. Here's senior designer Earl Gutnik, who has been there over thirty years: "I think it was a transition for me as an artist and design person. To paint the painting alone is the ultimate; but that's not what the visitor's here to see. They're here to see the product of what we're doing. And they don't know how messy it is, how hard it is. In fact, it looks seamless. And that's how we know when it's good, is it's totally believed without any question."

So what is it: what elaborate fabrication are these people offering? An exhibition: a theater for engaging people in the pulse of history.

There are four permanent exhibitions on view at the Minnesota History Center: *Grainland*; *Weather Permitting*; *Open House*; *and Minnesota's Greatest Generation*. Each exhibition is built on a set of stories. Each has at its core a "destination experience"—a haptic, immersive, surprising moment that kicks the perception of the surrounding objects up a notch and makes visitors into participants curious to learn more. That is the catalytic moment the MNHS teams strive for. The experience can be as simple as having kids climb through a maze of wooden compartments in a miniature grain elevator, or as complex as watching a media show that plunges visitors into an unnerving virtual life-or-death moment.

"The [media] shows are not a vehicle for delivering the didactic information. The shows are merely there for creating that emotional connection," says Media Producer Jesse Heinzen. "To get them receptive to . . . the didactic information that they're going to get in the rest of their visit here," adds Rich Rummel, another MNHS veteran. Preparing the Velcro ground. Facts can attach later.

In *Weather Permitting* and *Minnesota's Greatest Generation*, the vicarious experiences are particularly extreme—even life-threatening. In the first, you hunker down in a storm cellar, looking out a thin slit of window high in the wall at what appears to be ground level, while a tornado rages overhead and outside: wind howls, trees fall, lights fail, radio communication is cut off. In the second, you are flying with a crew of fellow paratroopers over the English Channel on D-Day, about to drop into battle amid the hail of enemy gunfire—if you can even make it that far. It's called "This Is Hell."

These media show moments "are signature experiences for young people," says Wendy Jones, who oversees education, public programs, and visitor services. She too, is an old-timer, having been at the History Center since it opened in 1992.

The staff is clear about the History Center's core audience; they are designing a multi-generational family experience. And sometimes a school experience. Either way, taking advantage of kids' natural curiosity and energy to the point of encouraging them to touch things, climb through them, plop down on beds that collapse, and open oven or refrigerator doors—this is the essence of their design practice. The History Center is devoid of docent-led lecture tours; it is permeated instead with "controlled chaos"—the gleeful shrieks and calls of kids' investigating and poking around on their own.

This spontaneous excitement reminds us of the City Museum and its exploration/play mandate. While the History Center retains these play-like virtues, its emphasis on imparting information—emotionally, cognitively, and experientially—means it remains more museum than amusement park.

For History Center director Dan Spock, you might say this was in his genes. He started out designing exhibits in a children's museum where he learned that "good intentions just don't cut it. Although good intentions are always *necessary* in creating programs for your audience, they're never sufficient."[1]

"You look to the visitors for cues as to what they want in an exhibit," agrees MNHS educator Annie Johnson. "It's almost like if you think about the exhibit as being this great big conversation piece—dynamic, in real time," says Spock. "You're moving through it and it's stimulating conversation or thinking all the time."

Johnson continues: "We find it's much more effective and enjoyable for people to walk through and experience the things themselves and have conversations within their group . . . whether it's grandparents and grandchildren or high school friends."

Of course, for these conversations to erupt naturally, you need to have engaging objects and narratives. The MNHS team speaks of two types of collections: physical objects and stories. They especially seek out the power of first person testimony, often gleaned from oral histories. "Stories are arti-facts," says Rich Rummel. "Preserve those words like 3-D materials and present them in a way visitors can appreciate."

In the exhibition *Open House: If These Walls Could Talk*, they took this approach to an extreme: there is only one object from the Minnesota Histori-cal Society's collection in the whole show. The galleries reproduce an actual home in St. Paul—one that was successively inhabited over more than a century by German, Italian, African American, and Hmong families. Visitors proceed from the upper middle class parlor of the original German phar-macist homeowners into the sub-divided apartments of the rooming house it became, witnessing traces characteristic of each family and the period in which it lived. As visitors move through the rooms, lifting casserole lids and opening drawers, they discover photos or cards with captions containing snippets of story.

"One of our biggest considerations," says Spock, "is 'What's the hook?' How do people get engaged with the past? Families are a near-universal experience. So we began with a home: one ordinary home that would have a bunch of real stories in it. We didn't do real objects," he says. "We did real stories."

By contrast, in the exhibition *Minnesota's Greatest Generation*, the His-tory Center organizers saw an opportunity to collect oral histories and

Figure 7.1 Minnesota History Center: *Open House*. A domestic interior with original stories, not original artifacts.

Figure 7.2 Minnesota's Greatest Generation: set portraying a dry cleaning shop, displaying uniforms and garments worn in the 1960s.

memorabilia from members of the World War II generation while they were still alive and feeling the need to pass on their stories to future generations. In this exhibition, there are literally cases full of recently acquired collection objects that evoke moments in the lives of the generation that was born in the 1910s and 1920s. As at Ruhr, we experience the power of humble objects.

"I think just about every artifact in that exhibit has a chunk of story attached to it on the exhibit label," says Annie Johnson. That makes for a profusion of labels, and even if each one is only a paragraph or two in length, it still may feel like too much to read.

Through audience research, the MNHS staff has learned to manage their expectations. They know, for instance, that the average visitor spends approximately twenty minutes in an exhibition—including the seven or more minutes for the media show. There is no expectation that visitors will read every label. The approach seems to be: if any of these objects attracts your attention, you will be able to learn something more about it. The artifacts in the case are just so many lures: visual hooks, each with a little cognitive bait attached.

Media presentations do not have to be over-the-top expensive. The History Center's creative producers know they will never have a budget to compete with Disney. In fact, one of the Center's most popular shows, *Home Place, Minnesota* (which closed in 2012), depended on nothing more than simple "scrim tricks": veils, mirrors, and centuries' old Pepper's Ghost effects that continued to enchant kids and adults well into the computer game generation. If you ask the staff why *Home Place*—originally slated to remain open for only six months—lasted for twenty years, they'll tell you that above and beyond the "cheap tricks done well" aspect of their métier, it depended on the power of story.

"Start with the story," says Jesse Heinzen. "It has to work as a radio play," adds Rummel. "You have to listen to it and stay engaged the whole time. And if it's really cool, then you have to say 'Okay, what do I see when I'm listening to this that allows me to stay focused on what I'm listening to?' You're enhancing the experience, somehow. You're creating the appropriate environment, the context."

How to evoke the defining experience for *Minnesota's Greatest Generation*: the trauma of World War II? Suspecting it would resonate with veterans from America's many wars, the MNHS team came up with "This is Hell." It is worth quoting at some length Director Dan Spock's reflections on this dramatic and immersive experience:

> From a philosophical standpoint, I thought one of the ideas that you want to get across is that being in war is not so much where you get to control the terms of it or where you are the predator, although there's an aspect of that; but the overriding impression that people get from war, the big wakeup call when you're actually a warrior, is that you could be killed at any time.
>
> And that you are really out of control of the situation for yourself. That as good as you are, as well trained as you are, as funny as you are, as athletic as you are, as inherently good a person as you are, or clever or whatever—funny, handsome—you know, it's still ultimately the luck of the draw, whether you're going to survive or not, if you're facing combat.
>
> And so the idea kind of formed, of both bringing home the perfect helplessness and terror that you feel in war as a warrior, and then the enduring sadness and grieving that you feel for having survived; and not just to have survived combat, but to be a survivor of a loved one or somebody who was lost.
>
> We worried a lot about whether veterans would be disturbed by . . . the realism of it. So we did a cardboard mockup of it with a test track early on, and they all gave us the thumbs up. It was really pretty interesting. Yeah. They were like, "This is really so important. You need to do this." So, yeah. And they were saying things like, "Having my family see this will help them understand why I've been the way I am my whole life."

Sometimes it's not "just the facts" that matter most.

This brings us back to the History Center's underlying goal: exhibits as goads to conversation—especially between kids and their parents, grandparents, or friends. Spock laments that our formal education system "kills the joy of learning." Here at the History Center, the topics may be tough, but at least the environment is safe. In fact, Spock and his team feel they have succeeded not when visitors come away with a pre-digested lesson, but when people are full of their own questions and reaching some new and unanticipated, but quite personal, insight.

"I've basically come to the conclusion that all museum-going is a form of play," says Spock. "And if you're in harmony with that as a museum maker, then people appreciate it a great deal. And I think people tend to think that the opposite of play is seriousness. But I think, really, the opposite of play is drudgery. When museums play on the voluntary nature of museum going, they always succeed." In exhibits like *Minnesota's Greatest Generation*, we come to appreciate the full valence of the term "serious play."

Co-Creating the Story: Inviting Silenced Voices into the Gallery to Evoke "The U.S.-Dakota War of 1862"

In Minnesota, history is still very much alive. In fact, the "Indian War" of 1862 is still being played out on the walls of a room behind the scenes at the History Center in St. Paul. Come. Lift the heavy brown curtain. You will find an entire set of galleries—one of two sets, in fact—where exhibitions are in development, in real time, at full

Figure 7.3 Minnesota History Center: exhibition prototyping.

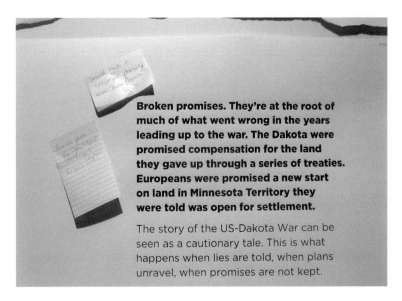

Figure 7.4 Minnesota History Center: two comments left by Dakota Indians. The one at the top says: "Should have a phrasing stronger than 'Broken Promises.'"

scale. These are not miniature mock-ups, or CAD software renderings. Rather, splayed across the walls are grainy visuals and rough mock-ups of wall texts, printed out on large sheets of paper and taped up with no concern for finish. What should they say? What is the logic of the sequence? What has been left out? That is what the exhibition team is trying to determine.

The exhibit developers have asked for input from members of the local tribes—descendants of the warriors who fought the state militia and the Union Army, and who... who, along with their families, were herded into camps where they fell sick or were forced into programs of de-culturation. Staff handed out Post-its saying: Tell us how to tell it. What are we getting wrong? Can you identify the people in this old photo? Leaving a notebook on a side table, they asked for longer reflections. Away from the museum, the staff reached out to people in the Indian community long before they ever asked them into the building. They are aware that the MNHS itself was complicit in this tragic series of events; some of its founders led the militias that fought the wars, and their descendants, too, live on in the community today.

So the museum is building relationships. Healing community. On one level, these galleries are just a byproduct, a visible sign of a negotiation in progress. The real work is going on in conversations—both out in the community and here behind the scenes. Eventually, there may be agreement or at least a new level of understanding. There may even be an exhibition.

Key Takeaways

1. The museum prioritizes visitor engagement over the showcasing of collections: they will only use an object if it advances the story. Visitor engagement does not necessarily require objects.
2. At the heart of each MNHS exhibition is a "destination experience": a moment designed to turn visitors from viewers to participants. Breaking the fourth wall turns the museum into a site of serious play, and it adds to visitor engagement.
3. The MNHS does not use the word "curator." Subject matter experts work as equals on collaborative teams alongside project managers, designers, media producers, and educators. A level playing field leads to creative solutions beyond the reach of any single expert.

Note

1 Spock was among the legion of museum leaders today who cut their teeth working under his father Michael at the Boston Children's Museum. And, of course, even his father Michael had a head start, for he was the son of Dr. Benjamin Spock, author of that most famed and oft reprinted post–World War II guide to parenting, *Baby and Child Care*.

III Reinvigorating Traditional Museums

Moving on, we consider three traditional collection-based museums, each recently reinstalled and reinvigorated. Located in non-tourist-destination cities (Detroit, Oakland, and Columbus), only one of them, the DIA, is world-renowned for its collection. As a result of their out-of-the-way locations, these museums share two interesting features: 1) the *need* to innovate—in particular, the need to continually recruit local return visitors and 2) the *freedom* to innovate—a chance to experiment outside of the limelight (in contrast to New York City, for example, where audience attendance is guaranteed but powerful boards and avid critical attention might thwart experimentation).

In these centers of innovation, we see three radically changed museums with strong leadership. By connecting to community, all three are dedicated to making real the mission of a visitor-oriented institution. While the particulars—of leadership style, audience research, in-gallery interpretive approaches, or team configurations—may vary, all three have made visitor research a new norm and created workflows to integrate this data into the exhibition development process. Additionally, with strong and seasoned directors at the helm, all three have stuck to their mission in the face of challenges of one kind or another.

These collection-rich museums embrace the notion of the museum as treasure house, but with an important contemporary revision: in the end, each prioritizes community in ways that convey: "This museum is *your* Treasure House."

8   Detroit Institute of Arts
Reinventing a Landmark
Museum with and for Visitors

The Detroit Institute of Arts, an encyclopedic art museum with a world-class collection, had to unlearn many of its time-honored practices in order to become more accessible. Staff responded to the leadership of their director, Graham Beal, who called for change. They also responded to the community around them, which had been radically impacted by economic challenges since the 1960s.

Beal takes seriously the notions of both deskilling and reskilling. Assuming the authority required to make change, he has not been afraid to take a firm stand, trumping curatorial authority and practicing "The buck stops here" when needed.

Ultimately, his institution rose to the challenge of connecting to community by transforming its galleries, programs, and overall approach to its visitors. In the process, while some disenchanted staff departed, the curators and interpretive specialists who stayed learned to take on new roles and listen to each other in new ways. They accepted guidance from internal and external teams. They developed new ways of telling stories, and they institutionalized feedback systems to gauge their success or make way for further improvements.

•

Everyone knows that decorative arts galleries from centuries past are a bore: the cases of porcelain and silver, the tapestries and furnished rooms that visitors walk by on their way to the Van Goghs and Monets. Yet at the Detroit Institute of Arts, we find something different: as we enter an upper level gallery, we are confronted by a periwigged portrait on a sign, placed at waist height. It reads:

> Much of the art in this suite was made before the French Revolution for European aristocrats who lived grandly, luxuriously, fashionably.
>
> The works of art help reveal how the privileged few wiled away their days and how they perceived others in the world.

This is a decisive departure from the normal Museum Voice of unreserved praise. We look around with new eyes. The world of privilege has been

Figure 8.1 Detroit Institute of Arts: *Splendor by the Hour* in the European decorative arts galleries.

named, challenged, and therefore relativized. We see luxurious works of art cast against their human cost. Permission has been granted to reconsider their value. Museumgoers are freed from the classic stance of unquestioning admiration. Reality has been rendered more complex—and inclusive.

That chased silver tureen with the hare, mushrooms, and wild boar is magnificent. That other silver lid sculpted with game birds, fish, and flowers. Each piece is more extravagant than the last. How could people have the means or the desire to surround themselves with so much bling? Another text cues us:

> This was a time of sumptuous living for aristocratic men and women. They enjoyed lavish lifestyles and developed elaborate rituals for their daily activities, from getting dressed to drinking a glass of wine. For even the most mundane tasks, only the finest luxury objects could touch their fingertips.

As visitors, we don't have to like it; we're just fascinated by all this evidence of decadence, knowing the end is going to come with a slice of the falling blade:

> Ultimately, this level of extravagance could not be sustained. As the upper classes grew more self-indulgent, the lower classes grew poorer

and more oppressed. Finally, on July 14, 1789, the citizens of Paris triggered a revolution that would transform the political systems of France, Europe, and beyond.

We know the outcome. Lessons of income inequality ring as true today as they did in the late eighteenth century, especially in a city that has fallen on hard times, and was but recently a bastion of automotive wealth. In the early to mid-twentieth century, the labor of Detroit's factory workers enabled the titans of the city to live like kings—and to acquire these objects that had once been owned by European royalty. Wealthy collectors with names like Ford and Dodge became founding patrons of the DIA we see today. Indeed, it is the objects they accumulated that comprise many of these exhibits.

In each of the subsequent galleries, part of an exhibit dubbed *Splendor by the Hour*, the story unfolds like a novel; we are invited to "step back in time . . . and experience some of the luxuries that made moving through the morning, afternoon, and evening a continuous delight for the aristocracy." Visitors now get to share in the circadian splendor of this decadent and doomed life. Room by room, moment by moment, we move through an aristocrat's day. We are even invited to take a seat as a banquet is laid out before us, a video projected onto the table surface using . . . the very same silver and porcelain that surrounds us in the display cases. The patter of French voices—first the servants, then the gentry arriving and taking their

Figure 8.2 Detroit Institute of Arts: *Splendor by the Hour* video banquet.

seats—invite us on a virtual culinary adventure, embedding us in the lives of these objects and inserting these objects into our lives.

Course by course, the meal is vividly evoked, offered to us in all its color, extravagance, and refinement. Our senses are bathed by the sights and by the sounds of the guests' conversations and the clinking of silver on fine china as virtual gloved hands serve each new dish and others—our surrogates—eat those presently before us. Alongside, the wall panel announces:

> Dinner culminates with dessert—the most sumptuous part of the meal. Pyramids of candied fruits and sweets and coolers of ice cream transform the table into a sugarcoated tablescape, reviving the appetites of the guests.

Transforming the table into a sugarcoated tablescape: the richness of metaphor is so far removed from the standard museum label that it bears repeating. These novelistic wall texts and the immersive, inviting video installation are exemplars for bringing distant times—and the objects that survive from them—back to life.

Visitor-Centered Interpretation Techniques

The DIA staff fundamentally reinvented the model for European decorative arts galleries when they designed and developed *Splendor by the Hour*. In fact, therein hangs a tale of an institution bent on reinventing itself—and a director convinced that no real innovation could happen without first changing the traditional process for developing exhibitions.

During the complete reinstallation of the DIA's galleries in 2002–05, with no need to look for outside loans, the museum looked instead for fresh perspectives on how to connect its world-class collection with an expanded and far more diverse public. In the process, they tested and changed not only received ideas but the museum's voice and the ways in which it communicated with its visitors.

Research revealed that many of the people they hoped to attract saw themselves as outsiders to the institution. Director Graham Beal tells the story:

> People [would] start the conversation by saying, "The museum is elitist; it's like a private club. I don't feel comfortable there." And when you say, "Well, okay, do you think the museum should be more like a shopping mall? I mean, you feel comfortable there." The answer is, "Oh no, no, no. The museum is special." So they want the museum to be special, but they want to belong.

In order to overcome this gulf, this outsider intimidation, Beal assembled teams from the DIA's own in-house staff—some trained, but importantly, many unschooled in art history. It was the latter group, staff members from departments like Marketing, Finance, and Operations—who, in the words of Director of Marketing Pam Marcil "obviously loved the museum"—that Beal was particularly depending on. Over a period of eighteen months, the teams collaborated with the curators; they provided feedback on which stories about the artworks interested them and therefore might qualify for selection as a "Big Idea" around which a gallery presentation could be built.[1] In this initial stage of the exhibition development process, staff stood in for those outsiders who avoided visiting the museum for fear of feeling excluded.

The radical departure here was that for the first time, it was no longer the sole province of the curators to decide the most important things to say about an artwork or gallery. In the words of the DIA's curator of contemporary art, Becky Hart:

> M. would ask questions that on one level, could seem very simplistic; and maybe at another time, we would've thought of them as naïve. But M. was typical, too, of a lot of people who come to the museum, who are intelligent people. Because of the questions that M. would ask . . . we couldn't take for granted that everybody gets this.
>
> I think a lot of times with museums, we've been more interested in what our colleagues, especially other art historians [think], and how we were perceived in the field—as opposed to always [focusing on] what our audience thought of us. We figured they'd come along anyway.
>
> Curators and educators have a metanarrative . . . the canon of art history . . . and having to explain that to other people, we learned that there were other stories. And so I thought that that was really a big advantage of the process.

In this re-visioned process, the curators had a new role: as resource people, experts who could tell innumerable stories about the artworks in their area. For its part, the museum team voted the stories up or down, and then sent the ones with the most resonance on to the director and his steering committee for final approval. In the words of curator of African American Art Valerie Mercer: "He basically didn't want the same old think . . . Mainly, I felt Graham did not want us to deal with the collection in the traditional, typical way."

Once a "Big Idea" was approved, interpretive educators developed questionnaires for the curators in order to draw out relevant stories and information about the artworks under consideration. The curators researched and wrote extensive responses, but—in an interesting and highly controversial twist—did not get to write the actual object labels or wall texts. Beal felt it was absolutely essential to wean the institution from its established emphasis on art historical verities and its tendency towards an academic, even pedantic, tone. And yet, perhaps cognizant of the radical reversal of power dynamics he had launched, rather than give the educators the label-writing task, he outsourced it completely. The sequence went like this: based on a gallery's big idea, educators prepared questions designed to elicit learning outcomes; curators then wrote extensive responses based on their research and knowledge of the objects; and finally, the whole package was sent out to one of a dozen freelance label writers scattered around the country. Laurel Paterson, the DIA's Director of Development, notes:

> We were very consistent in our message to the community that the museum was not any longer, or could not be perceived any longer, as an enclave of curatorial perspective; that we were really there to serve the visitors; that we were welcoming to novice visitors.

Once the big ideas had been developed by the in-house teams and interpretive materials had been prepared, the next step was to test them with visitor panels: carefully selected groups of community members representing target audiences the museum hoped to welcome when it reopened. These panels were comprised entirely of local residents whom the museum recruited through a market research firm and effectively "hired" as consultants. The panel process represented an ongoing engagement on the part of both the panelists—who were paid to attend periodically and advise—and the museum. More importantly, since the museum leaders hoped to broaden visitorship beyond their existing audience, it was essential to include open-minded non-visitors in the mix as well. (See Appendix C: Make-up of DIA Visitor Panels.)

Visitor panels are both like and unlike focus groups. Both are recruited to match target audience profiles, but in the museum world, focus groups typically only meet once, with museum observers hidden behind a one-way mirror. In contrast, the DIA's visitor panels met periodically, and the curators and interpretive staff sat around the periphery of the room, within view. Over time, visitors, prospective visitors, and staff became familiar with each other. The staff came to know these specific members of their community, listen to them, and rely on them—even as the panelists become increasingly invested in the success of the museum's efforts to communicate with people like themselves.[2]

Each three-hour session was structured down to the minute. Some segments were devoted to previewing gallery designs—in actual physical space when possible; if not, via a PowerPoint presentation. Panelists were asked to rate their first impression of a gallery and how it made them feel on a Likert scale from Comfortable to Uncomfortable, Inspired to Uninspired. At another point, they might be asked to compare different object label treatments, both for graphic appeal and for tone of voice. Presented with an array of six or eight different label approaches, visitor panels helped teams select the angle most likely to connect with viewers. In the words of Daryl Fischer, the consultant who organized and conducted these sessions in tandem with DIA staff, "Roles shift as visitor panelists assume the role of experts in the visitor experience; staff assume the role of listeners."

Copious data emerged from each session; each panelist filled out a questionnaire cued to the evening's activities; these answers were subsequently tallied, analyzed, and—along with a transcript of the entire session—were discussed in depth by museum staff.

Evaluator Matt Sikora described the staff commitment necessary to make the most of this process. First, the periodic, deadline-driven, cross-departmental production crunch that preceded each convening of a visitor panel and included content research, development of interpretive resources, and graphic design mockups. Next, sitting in on the panel session itself and absorbing the visitors' feelings and comments firsthand in real time. Finally, studying and discussing the data generated at each session:

> and then they had to read all of the transcripts. There was no report that was generated for visitor panels; they read the transcripts. They were given a set of filters, you know, four or five questions with which to read the transcripts . . .

- SURPRISES: comments that made you think differently about something
- BRIGHT IDEAS: comments that led you to new ideas that you'd like to consider, explore, experiment with
- VISITOR VALUES: basic needs and expectations that helped you understand what they want out of their museum experience
- CONNECTIONS: ways people connect personally with the works, and between artworks across the collection

> And then the teams would actually then meet with Daryl for about half a day, four hours, and go through and put up on sticky notes, what their responses to those were, and do affinity diagrams.

These methods of gathering visitor input were the beginning of empathic learning: training staff to listen closely to, and identify with, the predispositions of their public. At the same time, staff members were learning to work interdepartmentally in a far less hierarchical way than they ever had before. The museum was reinventing itself and its processes at the same time. Not surprisingly, some curators got onboard, others let themselves be dragged along, and still others got out. For curators who felt that asking visitors what they wanted was a fundamental betrayal of their scholarly responsibility, amounting to nothing more than pandering to the public, the DIA was no longer a comfortable place to work; for those who felt scholarly attention to collections could be matched with empathic attention to audience—the better to achieve the DIA's mission of helping each visitor find personal meaning in the artworks—this was an exciting if occasionally overwhelming adventure.

New Forms of Gallery Interpretation

Visitor panels proved useful in testing big ideas, museum voice, and new ways of providing interpretive support for looking at artworks just in time, right in the galleries. They helped the DIA prototype and develop a number of interpretive techniques, including two which are rarely seen in other museums: "pull-out panels" and "layered labels."

Pull-out panels are freestanding didactic signs floating above Plexiglas stands at waist height with each panel reproducing a specific artwork. The image includes circled highlights, each keyed to a short call-out commentary. The panels are perfectly adapted to iconographic analysis, fostering close attention to both the whole and its parts. An analog version of hotspots on

Figure 8.3 Detroit Institute of Arts: "pull-out panel." The darker ovals each connect to a short commentary.

a computer touchscreen, these signs silently perform the role of a gallery guide—or for that matter, an art historian with a laser pointer—permanently placed directly in front of the work. In educator Jennifer Czajkowski's words:

> What I like about those is it slows you down, and it models for visitors how to look at a work of art. You know, look at some of the details and then pull together the story. And I think that works really well, in not only slowing people down and getting them to look, but helping them understand that there are often stories, that there are things that they can figure out, puzzle through.

Layered labels are laminated magazine-style booklets in 8 1/2 x 11" format that visitors can flip through, also in the presence of an artwork. Positioned low enough to be legible to children or the wheelchair bound, they are set in a typeface large enough to read from standing height. Each booklet provides a short sequence of page spreads designed to rapidly scaffold the visitor into the complexity of a work through a combination of image and text. Like pull-out panels, layered labels are a way of overcoming the limitations inherent in a standard object label; they can present more information, comparison images, and context than a label can bear.

Figure 8.4a–c Detroit Institute of Arts: Richard Long's sculpture *Stone Line* with "layered label." In 8.4b, booklet is positioned on the Plexiglas stand to the right of the sculpture in the rear.

While clearly visible and easy-to-read from head-on, thanks to the transparent Plexiglas base, this didactic tool disappears when seen from across the room and does not distract from the viewing of the artwork.

What's more, neither of these interpretive tools requires an electrical plug. It's important to emphasize the value of just-in-time information provided to visitors at the point of their maximum curiosity, regardless of whether the information is analog or digital!

After so many innovations—ranging from the process for conceiving gallery themes to methods for delivering interpretive messages—the DIA understood there was yet another set of visitor-centered innovations that would prove essential: summative evaluations to get a sense of which approaches worked best, which less well, and how the DIA could continue to improve upon them. Museum consultant and evaluator Randi Korn calls this "living on the wheel of intentional practice," and the DIA had committed itself to "life on the wheel." With the funding they had received and their two in-house evaluators taking the lead, they brought in outside experts to perform a full battery of evaluations, both quantitative and qualitative.

Evaluation

The quantitative tests included extensive tracking and timing of visitors in twelve different sections of the museum. The results revealed the power of the approach taken with *Splendor by the Hour* and specifically, with its interactive video banquet. (Second only to the mummies in the Egyptian galleries, this exhibit exerted extraordinary holding power over DIA visitors.) Tracking and timing also proved the value of the "pullout panels," which encouraged attention to individual artworks and increased "dwell time."

Equally important and perhaps more revealing were the DIA's innovative qualitative evaluations. In the effort to test their success at fulfilling the museum's mission of "helping people find personal meaning in art," the museum recruited non-specialist visitors to walk through a specific set of galleries for twenty minutes and take pictures of objects or interpretive messages they found meaningful. Using what social scientists call a PhotoVoice method, staff then escorted these visitors to a computer station where their pictures were downloaded. Subjects were asked to share what about each image held personal meaning for them. Their comments were recorded using VoiceThread, a simple verbal annotation software, then transcribed and analyzed. While perhaps not as candid as an uncued "think-aloud,"[3] this technique came pretty close by catching visitors' internal monologues while they were still fresh.

As summarized by lead researchers Beverly Serrell and Marianna Adams, the results of the study point out three common meaning-making strategies—the sources of "Velcro" connecting people to specific artworks:[4]

> *Personal connection:* the artwork reminds them of something in their own lives. The hooks go into memory, association, and personal story.[5]

New discoveries: interpretive materials "add hooks to the hookless," drawing the viewer into the world of the artist and artwork through new insights.

Visual attraction: the artwork itself is enough of a "whammy" to draw viewers in and reward their gaze, without need for additional information or a personal story.

Interestingly enough, of these three strategies, only the second depends on interpretive material. Adams and Serrell put it this way: "the frequency [of] interpretation use in the galleries does not indicate anything about the quality of the experience the subjects had with art."[6]

The Community Responds

Thanks to director Beal's unwavering commitment to privileging actual visitor experience over traditional conventions of museum presentation and interpretation, and in spite of tremendous internal resistance and institutional inertia, the DIA found a way to fuse rigorous scholarship and empathic communication. As Beal told us, looking back and by implication, looking ahead:

> It's a lot of work—and you get a lot of resistance . . . But you have to do an enormous amount to get the individual to the art on their own terms, rather than your terms.

By extension, you have to do even more work to get a community as diverse as metropolitan Detroit to the art on their many and varied terms. In a testament to the DIA's efforts to listen to and build good will within this broad catchment of ethnicities, classes, and educational backgrounds, in 2012 the surrounding counties actually passed a tax to guarantee the institution's solvency. Subsequently, in the face of the city's much-publicized bankruptcy, the state, private foundations, and DIA patrons also stepped in to negotiate a "Grand Bargain" and help underwrite the city's waning pension funds rather than sell the treasures of a collection that they had, indeed, come to see as their own.

Key Takeaways

1. Unlearning time-honored practices is often necessary before a museum can more fully connect with its visitors. This process takes time and requires strong leadership.
2. Develop a culture of audience research: evaluation can involve both in-house staff and outside audiences. It's an iterative process.
3. Experiment with multiple modes of interpretive delivery—both analog and digital—in the galleries. As with DIA's decorative arts display, experimentation leads to teamwork and innovation.

Notes

1 "Big Ideas" are, in the words of Beverly Serrell, "a sentence—a statement—of what the exhibition is about . . . with a subject, an action, and a consequence." Beverly Serrell. *Exhibit Labels: An Interpretive Approach*. Walnut Creek: AltaMira, 1996, p. 1.

2 This can actually present a pitfall to the success of the process. Consultant Daryl Fischer points out that after several sessions, the panel no longer provides the "outsider" feedback for which they have originally been convened. At this point, she suggests the panel should be disbanded and a new one recruited. (Daryl Fischer. Personal communication, February 2014).

3 Adapted from social science, think-alouds are an open-ended museum research method that aims at making explicit that which is normally implicit in a person's behavior.

4 Adams and Serrell call these strategies Connection & Familiarity, Discovery & Learning, and Preference & Properties, respectively. See Marianna Adams and Beverly Serrell. *Phase 2 Summative Evaluation of DIA Interpretive Strategies*. Detroit: Detroit Institute of Arts, 2012.

5 This parallels the response of Abigail Housen's Stage 1 viewer in the Visual Thinking Strategies schema. Karin DeSantis and Abigail Housen. *A Brief Guide to Developmental Theory and Aesthetic Development*. New York: Visual Understanding in Education, Spring 2009.

6 Adams and Serrell. 2012, p. 5. This reminds us of Patterson Williams' comment after her years of interpretive scaffolding for visitors at the Denver Art Museum: "I want them to have *their* experience, each and every oddball one of them."

9   Oakland Museum of California

Including a Diverse Public

Under the direction of Lori Fogarty, OMCA is another collection-based museum that reinvented itself from the ground up. They embraced the challenges of working across disciplines, seeing that interpretive tools that meet audience needs in one area may be applied to another—for example, in art and natural history.

Honoring the questions of inexperienced museumgoers, OMCA changed its exhibition spaces to welcome the entire community. With new hires and a staff reorganization, they created interdepartmental teams to develop exhibitions and activities that make it clear that all Oaklanders (and for that matter, all Californians and visitors from beyond) are welcome.

Visitor research has informed every aspect of OMCA's new design. As a matter of routine practice, OMCA staff test ideas by informally putting them out in the galleries; an in-house idea isn't good enough until it's been vetted by visitors.

Informed by clear leadership, in Oakland—a non-destination city—we see a dramatically reinvigorated museum driven by the desire to connect to its diverse and growing community.

•

> "Stepping into [an] art exhibition can be like stepping into the middle of a conversation that began without you and is being conducted in a secret language."
> —Jaime Cortez, artist and guest writer, Oakland Museum of California

Cortez's plaint would not have come as a surprise to Pierre Bourdieu (the French sociologist of culture whose theory about high culture as a wedge that divides the classes was mentioned earlier). Overcoming this divide—these perceived "barriers to entry"—to make new groups of visitors feel welcome is indeed a challenge, one the Oakland Museum of California (OMCA) is facing head on. Oakland is one of the most diverse communities in America, with a population makeup 26% Caucasian, 28% African American, 25% Latino, 17% Asian, 2% American Indian, and 6% self-classifying as of two or more ethnicities. The OMCA is the result of the union of three different museums—one devoted to natural science, another to history, and a third to art—that came together in 1969 in a three-level building, bounded by city streets on one side, gardens on another. By the 1990s, the galleries and physical plant were sorely in need of a refresh; thanks to a museum and library bond issue passed by voters in 2002, OMCA had the wherewithal to act. The museum also had a new director in Lori Fogarty, recruited from the Bay Area Discovery Museum.[1]

The gallery redesign was already underway when Fogarty arrived; feeling the plans didn't go far enough in re-conceiving the relationship between the museum and its community, she pulled the plug. "We would have had some *really nice fonts*," she says wryly.

Fogarty's first order of business was to develop a more nuanced understanding of OMCA's community and its needs. By surveying gallery visitors and reaching beyond the museum's walls through an elaborate set of community advisory panels, the museum queried more than 3,300 people in three years. This research surfaced the following questions:

1.   Why are these works together in this area in this arrangement?
2.   Why is this even here in the museum?
3.   Whose point of view is this?
4.   What is this in front of me?
5.   What motivated the artist to make this? How was it made?
6.   But why does this matter? Where are the other perspectives?
7.   Is there a right way I'm supposed to look at this artwork?[2]

The list, as elementary as it seems, is worth its weight in gold, for these questions reveal that it's not just "Art" or "History" that's hard. *Museums* can be hard too, especially for those who don't think of themselves as insiders.

Honoring these questions—and the people who ask them—is an essential part of OMCA's mission. It makes explicit the tacit assumptions on which the exhibitions are built. In this vein, Barbara Henry, founding director of the refashioned interdepartmental team dubbed OMCA Lab, talked about what motivates her:

> It was really having this experience of not knowing how to appreciate a work of art, you know? And that's what drove me to study art history . . . I saw how I was able to make the transition and how powerful it was, that became my motivator to become an educator in a museum.
>
> My passion was the outsider. This is a public museum. It is really thinking for the people out there that—going back to the point where I felt alienated—kept me going.

Reflecting the belief that museums belong to everyone, OMCA's Philosophy of Interpretation specifies: "Decisions about audiences and programs should be consciously made . . . to ensure they do not, by default, exclude those who historically have felt museums to be inhospitable public places."[3] In the spirit of Judy Rand's "Visitor Bill of Rights" (reprinted on pages 5–6), OMCA recognizes that for many populations, museums have a long way to go before they are perceived as "safe."

As an interdisciplinary museum, OMCA benefits from a wider range of curatorial vocabularies and display strategies than most. As Director Fogarty states:

> There's not an assumption in a history museum that just putting an artifact out is enough—that if you just have it there, it speaks for itself. There's a knowledge in history museums that you have to provide the stories and the context and the experience, to understand what that gold nugget is or what that shovel is; where there's more of a sense in art museums that art speaks for itself. And so, you know, it doesn't need the context or the experience or the story.
>
> So I think what we've been able to translate from history museums is that freedom to say, "Yes, people need a point of entry. They need a context, they need some tools to help them understand."

Figure 9.1 Oakland Museum of California: "Cultures Meet" in OMCA's History galleries.

On the other hand, history museums can learn from art museums, too (as demonstrated by the Ruhr Museum's display techniques—see Chapter 6). OMCA Senior Art Curator René de Guzman:

> But sometimes an object can speak for itself and you just clear out and let the thing do what it does . . . Assuming you're in front of an awesome work of art, it's a great experience . . . where your jaw drops and you're much more engaged and ready to get deeper into this thing. And that seduction and that wow is really important to learn about.

OMCA presents an admirable example of just this sort of riveting juxtaposition in its history galleries, where in a darkened room, a plumed headdress dramatically confronts a Spanish colonial helmet.

The differences between history, science, and art museums have often extended to their exhibition development processes as well. For instance, prototyping is largely unfamiliar to the art world. Director Fogarty:

> When I was interviewed about our project by *ARTnews*, and I talked about prototyping, the writer said, "What is prototyping?"

To hear OMCA's senior curator of history Louise Pubols tell it, the traditional way of installing history exhibitions was not all that different from the process still common in art museums:

> The traditional way of doing it is, the curators do their bit, they hand it off, maybe they have a small discussion with the educator, maybe not. Maybe the educator just gets a little room in the corner; that's their little gallery. And then it gets handed off to the designers, who do their thing.

In contrast, OMCA has employed a team-based approach much like the Minnesota History Center's (see Chapter 7). OMCA adopted this evaluative, team-based approach for all three collections—history, natural sciences, and art. Implementing it was facilitated thanks to Fogarty's hiring of an outside consultant on the reinstallation project. Fogarty explains:

> Our process was more everybody's in the room together. You talk things through. It takes all day; you're exhausted at the end of the day. You think you've made a decision and then you come back tomorrow and it's—all bets are off and you're starting over again.
>
> But it also means that, you know, the designers are out there prototyping; you go and take a look at it. You like this, you don't like that; they're going to tweak it. They come back again with a new little build thing that they've done. You've got paper prototypes all over the place and cardboard prototypes all over the place, and everybody's kind of in the conversation together.

And it's not clear-cut and you don't know that you're really going to make it on time. So that's the part that's scary, I think. But you have to just sort of trust that this is the right process to get the best possible visitor engagement result.

Another typical distinction between history and art museums is that the former are frequently comfortable inviting visitors to contribute their experience and perspective directly into the galleries, whereas in art, "it's more viewed as 'What is the curatorial perspective?'"

Interdisciplinarity

OMCA Consultant Kathleen McLean speaks of how history and science museums can learn from art museums:

> Historians and scientists can often get really bogged down in the facts . . . and ignore the imagination. And I think the partnership with art is the celebration of the imagination and the freedom, the releasing people from their really rigid constraints and thinking.

She speaks too of how all disciplines are increasingly coming to recognize their interdependence:

> What's happening now, in this new kind of world, given the technology that we have to engage, is that environmentalists are talking to philosophers, are talking to artists, are talking to dancers, are talking to neurosurgeons, and they're finding common ground, and that common ground is actually where our new knowledge and wisdom is coming from.
>
> So it's a deep need in our society, to have history learning something from art and science learning something from history.
>
> And by keeping these boundaries separated, they actually create a false sense of knowledge that's actually an old—it's no longer useful for us.

These two tendencies—prototyping with formative evaluation along the way and inviting visitors to connect personally and creatively with the objects on view—were vividly exemplified in OMCA's Gallery of California Art through the activity that came to be called *You Are Here.*

It started out as a very different activity. Working in a small gallery "lab space" adjacent to the main galleries, interpretive staff started by installing four artworks that each showed a somewhat abstracted figure, next to which they posted a set of open-ended questions:

- Why do artists use different kinds of lines?
- Why do you think artists draw people in different ways?
- Can you draw a person using only three lines?

They put pads of sticky notes out. The questions were at once too abstract, too didactic, and too open-ended. Very few visitors responded, so they changed the set-up. In the second month, staff added a prop and a new prompt. Hanging a mirror on the wall, they wrote: *Draw yourself here.*

Suddenly, they had liftoff. It turned out colored sticky notes and pencils were all people needed to have a bout with simple self-portraiture. The museum had tapped into the then nascent contemporary culture of the "selfie"—this was 2007—and given people permission to *see* themselves, right there in the museum. The very place we normally reserve for the famous and important. The evaluation report insightfully surmises: "The activity needed to be personally relevant to be engaging." Now the sticky notes were flying: of 810 responses collected, three quarters were drawn.[4]

Of course, with this newfound success came new challenges. Office staff had to build in time to sweep through the Art Lab gallery twice a day to re-supply sticky notes and sharp pencils, and straighten up the space. The report states:

> One concern for both curators and educators was how to encourage visitors' personal expression through drawing without having hundreds of pieces of paper all over a section of the Museum.[5]

It was one thing to unleash a storm of pink and yellow wide-format Post-its all over the walls of a confined experimental space called an Art Lab; it would be something else altogether to have them compete with the muted tones of the collection of historical California portraits once the painting galleries were reinstalled. Another solution would have to be found.

The stickies had served their purpose: the quick cycles of prototyping, feedback, modification, and success had given both curators and educators (now called "experience developers") the confidence to move ahead.

Now, at the "People" wall in the art galleries, we find a salon-style array of portraits—of many sizes, shapes, and periods—returning our gaze. Some sitters are known and some not; some are painted by famous artists and others not. They were all fished out of storage. Except two.

Those two frames on the wall house luminous screens. They don't stand out much at first, but you see them because they're a bit brighter—*and they change.* Down to the left are two stools and up-turned touchscreens sticking out from the wall. On the first, a thumbnail array of portraits drawn by other visitors who have passed through. If you click on any one of them, it will reconstitute itself, before your very eyes, from Stroke One to the finish.

Figure 9.2 Oakland Museum of California: *You Are Here* in the California Portrait Gallery.

On the right, it's your turn. A gridded mirror sits on the wall before you, while the blank screen below displays a row of color swatches along its upper edge. Tap a color, look into the mirror, and start drawing with your finger.

What is it to make a self-portrait? Which lines do you make as you go? Which opportunities will you take along the way, which will you leave behind? What is the tone you wish to strike—or, having struck, to balance, change, accept, reject?

When visitors are done, they may look back at the screen to their left, and gaze with new curiosity and respect at the hundreds of compositions made by others who have sat in their place. Then they can look up at the wall to their right, hung with all those portraits pulled from "the morgue"—Storage— and see themselves as part of a flickering continuum, a community across time, of creators and observers.

The *You Are Here* interactive gets it right on many levels, among them:

- It is integrated into the gallery to which it refers.
- It provides its own seating—an implicit invitation to participate.
- Visitors participate at the level of their ability, across the spectrum of talent, style, and age.
- The left station models what the right station is doing—even as it provides a fascinating, "on deck" waiting space, where you can learn techniques by watching other people's drawings re-enacted.

- Visitors get immediate positive reinforcement, seeing their self-portrait appear briefly on the gallery wall when it's done, producing a personal, shareable souvenir with its own URL.
- Filters are in place; each portrait goes into a holding pool for vetting by museum staff before entering the permanent—and public—cycle.

OMCA's commitment to community has extended beyond interpretive strategies to encompass the kinds of exhibitions presented; increasingly, they reflect the diverse demographics of the community. Beyond the galleries, live programming has picked up the thread and amplified it; every Friday night, the museum hosts a block party with live music, dance lessons, a line-up of food trucks of many ethnic persuasions, a no-host bar for parents, creative activities for kids in the courtyard, and half-price admission to the galleries. In so doing, OMCA has turned itself into a lively town square in a city that did not have one, welcoming people of all ages and backgrounds: a safe place for families, elders, a date—you name it.

Key Takeaways

1. OMCA combines research and teamwork. Their innovation echoes that of the MNHS: subject matter curators work together with experience developers and evaluators to prototype exhibition engagement strategies and test them with a broad range of visitors.
2. The *You Are Here* activity springs directly from the museum's mission, making innovative use of participatory technology so visitors can see themselves and their creations literally belonging in the galleries. At the same time, they gain a greater appreciation of artistic technique. Carefully crafted activities such as these build personal connection.
3. OMCA is an interdisciplinary museum that, like Detroit, has reinvented its structure and working processes so inexperienced museumgoers feel welcomed, not intimidated.
4. OMCA provides another example of the innovations happening outside of major cities and tourist destinations.

Notes

1 Fogarty had previously served as deputy director of the San Francisco Museum of Modern Art.
2 Mary T. Faria. "Inviting Visitors into the Conversation about Art: Labels." In Barbara Henry and Kathleen McLean (Eds.), *How ~~We~~ Visitors Changed Our Museum: Transforming the Gallery of California Art at the Oakland Museum of California*. Oakland: OMCA, 2010, p. 37.
3 "Philosophy of Interpretation." Internal document reprinted in Henry and McLean 2010, A2–A5.
4 Like MNHS, OMCA values visitor experience so much that they have set aside a small public gallery space to actively prototype and evaluate visitor engagement

strategies. Art museums typically don't make this a priority. Museums won't go these lengths to understand their community's needs unless they really want to know.

5 Karen Nelson. "Seeing Ourselves in the Gallery of California Art." In Barbara Henry and Kathleen McLean (Eds.), *How We Visitors Changed Our Museum: Transforming the Gallery of California Art at the Oakland Museum of California.* Oakland: OMCA, 2010, p. 62.

10 Columbus Museum of Art
Museum as Community Living Room

Located in a heartland city without a strong tourist base, the Columbus Museum of Art (CMA) is another museum firmly committed to experimentation and inclusion. Understanding the need to cultivate relationships with the local community and foster return visitation, Director Nannette Maciejunes has adopted a mission of "Great experiences with great art for everyone," and the museum is finding ways to make good on that goal.

Maciejunes recognized the need to provide in-gallery support for visitors who lack her expertise. She also understood that it was incumbent on the museum to adapt rather then expecting the public to do so. The museum's commitment to visitors is evident throughout the institution from including visitor research as an integral part of exhibition design to the staff-wide belief that different kinds of "connectors" and installed interpretives are needed to reach a broad public. As it has reinvented itself to focus on community, the museum has also changed its ways of working. No longer driven exclusively by a curatorial mandate, new teams consisting of educators, curators, and other stakeholders now share the responsibility of crafting exhibitions that both inform and connect.

The CMA brings to life a re-visioning process we have seen elsewhere: a commitment to conscious hospitality with an emphasis on the museum as community living room.

•

"It's not like we lost our art history. It's just we don't feel that's more important than the people who walk in our door."
—Merilee Mostov, CMA's Chief Engagement Officer

In a gallery titled "The Changing Landscape," a young couple sits at a small round table before a painting by Arthur Dove. They are deep in conversation as their hands fit the final pieces into a jigsaw puzzle. It represents the painting that faces them on the wall. They have been here in this gallery—sitting, talking, looking, and fitting—for forty-five minutes. He is on leave from the army, and this is how they have chosen to spend their last day together.

Across the room is another small table, this one surrounded by a group of five teenagers, sitting a few feet from a Richard Long sculpture of stone blocks arrayed on the floor in concentric circles. The teens are playing with a set of small red and white stones on the tabletop, trying out different arrangements, talking and joking as kids do, thoroughly engaged.

It's Sunday at the Columbus Museum of Art; admission is free, and the community is connecting with the art.

Columbus is rated one of the 100 Most Livable Small Cities in America; it's a college town and a Big-10 sports town. It is not first and foremost an art town. One staff leader describes his brother's response to the CMA's pre-modern galleries: "They're just pretty pictures on the wall." That response changes when the subject turns to modern works: "Why do people paint like that?" he asks. "Why don't they just make it look real?" Among those of us trained in modern art history that objection may feel easy to dismiss; nonetheless it represents a mystified view still held by many, here and across the country.

If you're running an art museum in a small city without a perpetual influx of cultural tourists to support you, you have to turn to the population that is already there and say: how can we mean more to these people? Whether it's Columbus, Detroit, Oakland, or a hundred other cities and towns across America, tourism alone is not enough to drive the turnstiles. You have to think about new ways—beyond organizing blockbusters—to turn your local audience into return visitors.

CMA Director Nannette Maciejunes on the Unique Challenges Facing Regional Museums

What does a visitor-centered art museum look like? I think we're the last kind of museum to be asking that question. Because we are so object-oriented . . . We want a bigger audience. We want to grow our audience. But we haven't really grappled, in the art world, with what that means. I mean, it's easy to say: I want to grow my audience. And what you really mean is you want more people like me to come. And that's a finite number of people. And in the United States, I'd say that's a pretty small finite number of people. And it's not enough to sustain an art museum and it's not enough to make the museum relevant to the community. So I think that's hard, grappling with what that means. What do you mean you want to grow your audience?

But we've got to be better at listening to our visitors and understanding their anxieties and breaking down those barriers. And I guess I'm for anything that moves that agenda along. And I think if we don't move that agenda along, we're going to see—in regional museums, at least—an increasing isolation out of the mainstream of what people in that city are doing.

> I don't think that's a threat or an issue for large cities, where you're doing the top ten things in New York. You're not going to go home and say you didn't go to the Museum of Modern Art or the Met. But they're more than willing not to come to the art museum in their own city. And I think that you're going to see a lot of the more interesting thinking coming out of regional museums, because we have a different challenge . . . We need to activate those audiences and engage people in storylines that they can relate to. I mean, art has always been about storytelling. That's one of its things.
>
> And how do we connect people to those stories? Because I think what is going to happen if we don't do this is, people begin to ask you why you're spending those resources, those very valuable resources in your community, to sustain these objects. If the objects don't mean something to us, in our contemporary lives, have relevance and value in a contemporary context, why are you spending the resources to do that? And I think that's the bottom-line question. And regional museums have got to answer that effectively.

In the CMA's case, the response began with a new mission statement: *Great experiences with great art, for everyone*, put in place by CMA Director Nannette Maciejunes. That led to an engagement with Joe Heimlich, a seasoned evaluator in science museums, zoos, and history museums. Heimlich's COSILab offered his team's services to a number of regional art museums in Ohio, including CMA. Maciejunes was quick to recognize the value of this offering.

And so began the undertaking. CMA Director of Education Cindy Foley remembers her own "Aha!" moment, as Heimlich tasked an interdepartmental group with finding three measurable outcomes for visitors to an upcoming exhibition. "I think the start of our process began with understanding what an outcome was and what we needed to accomplish in order for our visitors to take away meaning, personal meaning, as well as understanding."

Heimlich's focus on designing for specific outcomes seemed simplistic to some, and it surfaced worries about dumbing down. Not surprisingly, curators resisted backing off all the important art history data they wanted to impart. Catherine Evans, Chief Curator at the time, puts her struggle with understanding the implications of Joe's approach this way:

> It was a long process to incorporate and start to really understand: what does this mean? I come from a really traditional museum background; it was very conservative. It's like: This is dumbing down. How do we wrestle with those things? I have to say that having someone from the outside is so important.

Their first outcome—that visitors would understand that Op Art was an important art movement—was pretty flat-footed. Over time, other outcomes have become part of the CMA's shared vocabulary:

- Critical thinking: Visitors think, analyze, reflect, compare . . .
- Close observation: Visitors look with intentionality at, pay close attention to . . .
- Conversation: Visitors have conversations, share, tell, write about . . .
- Collaboration: Visitors work together to . . .
- Experimentation: Visitors experiment, play, make, try . . .
- Personal relevance: Visitors make connections to their lives.
- Awareness: Visitors have a greater understanding or curiosity about . . .

If the outcomes are the ends, it still remains to identify the means. Through extensive gallery observation, creative project lead Merilee Mostov determined that only 5–12% of CMA's visitors actually read the wall texts and labels that constitute most art museums' default means of communicating a message.

For an institution whose brand tagline is: *Art Speaks: Join the conversation,* this was a disheartening finding. Curators and directors are used to relying on their wall labels to represent the museum voice. If people aren't even reading what you write, you have to find another way to engage. As Maciejunes reports: "And then, you say: 'Well, they *should* read the text panels.' And you can either just sit here and argue with yourself . . . or you can decide another way to engage them in this process."

Maciejunes is cognizant of the tacit rules and expectations art museums place on their visitors—"There's the written rules and the unwritten rules"—and she has seen how museums' standard operating procedures can lead to intimidation and avoidance. Wall texts, for example, pass the litmus test as a universal baseline of museum practice. But *what if* most people don't read them—and we still want to get our ideas across? Maciejunes suggests that's the time to come up with fresh approaches to supplement the labels instead of saying, "Gosh, we really love this tool and we want to keep using it, even though it doesn't work."

CMA's commitment to experimentation kicked in. They started with reading rooms: "But you know, we moved from having the reading room at the end to putting it in the middle, and from there to breaking it into these segments," says curator Catherine Evans.

In this way the Connector was born, and it often bypassed reading altogether. In Merilee Mostov's words, connectors are "any strategy that connects people to the art, besides the art itself." They range from design decisions like wall color to gallery furniture, and from object labels to games, activities, and occasionally multimedia. They are the hooks that give Velcro to a specific work and make it stick. Mostov and her colleagues have invented connectors in every shape and size: custom-crafted gameboards themed to the works on view, jigsaw puzzles of paintings, visible voting polls that ask you to rank one painting against another, "Join the Conversation" Post-it bulletin boards—you name it (see sidebar). And they are always paired with seating and placed right in the galleries, among the artworks.

Connectors

As part of CMA's exhibition development process, a cross-departmental team meets to develop the gallery's interpretive strategies. First they identify the exhibition's Big Idea and Learning Outcomes, then they brainstorm Connectors to triangulate the art and the visitors and to help foster an "Aha!" experience. A connector can be as simple as a seat or a label, or it can be a more interactive project that elicits the visitor's own creativity. Here are some ideas from their toolbox:

- Seating
- Object label
- 75-word text panel
- Print handout
- Cellphone tour stop
- Timeline
- Map
- Drawing activity
- Building activity
- Picture/photo on the label
- Puzzle
- Cell phone scavenger hunt
- Conversation board
- Visual poll
- Music
- Video
- Books/reading materials
- Live programming

It helps that the galleries themselves are thematically organized, each one designed to express a Big Idea. "We treat every gallery as an exhibition," says Mostov. That requires a cross-departmental effort to develop learning outcomes for the gallery and brainstorm an appropriate connection strategy. "If we need to really nail a particular outcome, we often have to address it more than one time, in multiple ways. So it has to be in the label copy, but it also has to be in other formats."

Take polls, for instance: visitors drop wooden tokens into a visible voting station made of Plexiglas columns in response to a question posed on a label. Here's an example:

> Claude Monet painted some of the landscapes displayed on the wall in front of you. His contemporaries made the others.
>
> All of these artists and others like them, who later were labeled Impressionists, paid special attention to the changing light, shadows, and colors around them. They sought to capture a truthful yet modern depiction of what they saw.
>
> Using a wooden chip, vote for the painting that you think best captures the impressionist's intention.

The actual physical polling stations can be changed out with new questions, relocated in any gallery, and repainted to match the walls. Why voting stations? Mostov explains:

> The two goals I'm trying to accomplish are to get people to stop and slow down and look at a work of art—if I'm going to make a choice among these seven paintings, I'm going to have to look at each one—and to provoke conversation, because we know people come in social groups.

Figure 10.1 Columbus Museum of Art: Impressionist landscapes with visible voting poll.

The Columbus team practices constant ad hoc informal evaluation. It may not always be as systematic as they might wish:

> So to me, successfully evaluating in a gallery . . . we would take photographs of all the connectors—including the label copy, the text panel. When people came out, we would have an intern standing there, show them pictures and say, "Point to each one that you participated in." We'd [ask them to] show us, "*What* did you think the big idea was?" We'd record *their* big idea. And then we would see, did they get close to the big idea? Which of the connectors were successful in helping them get there?

Mostov admits they don't always get that far, but they have no fear of stepping into the galleries on a daily basis to watch visitors and engage them in conversation. She says: "I'm all about talking to people. I do that a lot. I just go up to people and talk . . . And I love to go [have] conversations with people and hear from them, good or bad, and find out."[1]

So say the educators/experience developers. But what about the curators? Some are very much on board. One curator says:

> I find it inspiring. I know the game is changing. I don't see a way back. I don't see the value in that. . . . You know, it's not throwing the baby out with the bath water; it's really about using all of that talent to its best advantage, in a world that doesn't know a lot about art history.

Ironically, it is in the constantly changing field of contemporary art that the greatest obstacles tend to arise. On the one hand, as Lisa Dent, then Columbus's curator of contemporary art, stated:

> I think it's difficult for a contemporary art curator in the last ten or twenty years, to not be thinking about how to explain or discuss this really complicated material to an audience, especially when there's no text around it and there's not a lot of information to be had.

On the other hand, there are challenges. For example, in their departure from the framed oil paintings and pedestal-mounted sculptures that have characterized western art since the Renaissance, contemporary artists have been trained to conceive of the entire gallery as their display space, fully under their control. Mostov comments:

> I think in the gallery with the most contemporary art, it has literally became an issue of space, because a few things that I wanted to do were in the middle of the gallery, on the floor. Where is the seating going to work? What is it going to be? And I think that that's the challenge with work, as it becomes less about painting on the wall.

Second, contemporary artists are, in most situations, still alive, and often they actively collaborate with the curators in what becomes an intimate working partnership. As a result, museums bend over backwards to accommodate and realize the artists' visions whenever possible. It takes a strong director to insist that the artist and curator factor in the museum's visitor-centered mission as part of the constraints informing their creative process. In the words of curator Dent:

> I'm really considerate about the artists that I invite to do an exhibition here. I really talk to them, I think about it. I have had artists choose not to do things here, after those discussions. You know, it started to worry me at one point, but I just thought, you know, this is the way this institution is going and either we commit or we don't.
>
> One thing that Merilee [Mostov] and I really learned is that the conversation needs to start really immediately. From the first conversation when I'm talking with the artist, to go over sort of our mission and what we do here and what that is, instead of doing it later, where it's a surprise and they're saying: "Hold on, I just worked on this whole thing and . . ." You have to do it. And just everyone's part of the team. People just want to be communicated with and included.

Dent points out that the visible voting polls raised alarm bells with certain artists:

> The voting booth has been incredibly divisive for me in conversations. It's just been something that I've had a lot of feedback around, [like] "people are looking at this cardboard representation and they're not looking at my painting, they're not looking at my work."

Gallery installation also becomes an exercise in group problem-solving and includes the curator, engagement specialist, and exhibition designer. A spirit of teamwork is key: how can they realize the curator and the artist's vision while still honoring the needs of visitors who are unfamiliar with modern art? The more challenging the art, the more the team has to exercise its own dual empathy—to both the artist and the viewer—and stretch to find a creative response. Dent has been impressed by just how game her interpretive colleagues have been to rise to the challenge:

> I was amazed that [I] still got great feedback from everybody and sort of had decided that again, I needed to really address these strange objects in the collection, like pieces of cardboard and foam, and wanted to present them, as opposed to focusing on some other really beautiful works— Agnes Martin. And felt really supported in that. You know, that people felt like, yes, we needed to sort of make the plunge and make a really challenging room for everybody.

The fewer "hooks" in the art, the more the museum is called on to supply the Velcro itself—including through the intelligence and sensitivity of the gallery assistants.

All agree that teamwork is an organizational learning process that is far from clear-cut. Sometimes it feels like navigating through a minefield, as the loss of a single clear, decisive voice raises frustration on the part of curators (who no longer serve as final arbiter) and defensiveness on the part of educators (who have now been given the mandate to meet visitor needs). In the words of Cindy Foley, Curator of Education:

> I would say there were moments of even, are we going down the right path? Now, what we tried to do—we tried to really base it on, well, how are the visitors? Are we noticing differences? Are we having the impact? Are we achieving a different experience that's a more meaningful experience, with visitors? And the more we did get that kind of feedback, the more we wanted. I mean, and so it did feed itself.

Chief Engagement Officer Mostov is quick to add that the way forward requires experimentation, and that each museum must find its own style and path. That path emerges from internal collaboration and dialogue with its community:

> I just think it's important to know that this is a messy process. This is not neat and tidy. This is not about one day waking up and saying, Oh, we ought to do what Columbus Museum of Art is doing. I think it's great that institutions are talking to one another and modeling on one another and figuring out what works for them, what doesn't work for them, because there is not one formula. And we're figuring it out as we go along, with as much information, as much openness as we possibly can.

Helping Newcomers—Both Kids and Adults—Learn Museum Protocol

On entering the Columbus Museum of Art, visitors are greeted by an unusual display: a trio of exhibits designed to engage and educate people who might be unfamiliar with museum manners and the riches of the collection. On one wall, a large screen displays a stop-motion animation in which colorful paper figures demonstrate "Museum DOs and DONTs." This light-hearted intro sums up in a minute the behaviors museums expect from their visitors: in the video, every *No* is accompanied by a clever and demonstrative illustration and there is a *Yes* to balance it out. As Mostov says:

> If we're inviting them and want them to be engaged in those galleries, then we also have another job ahead of us, which is to communicate behaviors and attitudes.

Figure 10.2a–e Columbus Museum of Art: five frames from the *MUSEUM DOs &*
   DON'Ts video.

To the left, a Conversation Board on the wall displays visitor and staff recommendations for what to see in the museum, each with a small picture of an artwork on it. Just below: paper, pencils, and an invitation to submit your own favorite at the end of your visit. Still further left on the same wall, a shelf sporting four upturned brass doorknobs (Figure 10.3).

Finally, visitors are invited to pick up cards headlined "Try This!" with prompts to consider when looking at the art in the galleries.

If you happen to be a family, staff might suggest you visit the "Wonder Room," a strikingly designed, multi-generational center for creativity that is part art gallery, part playground, and part maker space.

Figure 10.3 Columbus Museum of Art: child-friendly display demonstrates reason for "No Touching" policy.

Figure 10.4a–d Columbus Museum of Art: Wonder Room. Collection objects in glass display cases, while kids assemble mobiles and sculptures. Meanwhile, parents on nearby couches view videos presenting art projects they can do with their children at home.

Figure 10.5 Columbus Museum of Art: an intimate moment in the "Love and War" gallery.

What It Can Look Like When It's Right

There's so much right with this picture: visitors seeing themselves reflected in the art; use of a wall color to relieve the detachment of the white cube; comparative illustrations on the wall labels; a gallery overview panel to tell those who care to know why these works share a room together; and the fact that all of these connectors can remain present for those who need them even as they are discreet enough to remain superfluous to those who connect intuitively with an artwork.

Key Takeaways

1. Museums in cities that do not supply a steady stream of tourists need to cultivate a relationship with their local community and foster experimentation. Adapt to your public rather than expect them to adapt to you.
2. The Chief Engagement Officer holds new cross-functional teams accountable to the visitor-centered mission. This process can be messy and requires patience.
3. Recognizing that contemporary art is often bewildering to the local audience, the museum prepares artists by informing them of its visitor-centered approach in advance.
4. Welcome families and design for their specific needs.

Note

1 Mostov is not alone. In fact, more and more museums now employ paid or volunteer Gallery Guides (so named at OMCA; at Columbus they're called Gallery Assistants, and at the Van Abbe, Museum Hosts): staff members trained to engage with visitors about the exhibitions—either as part of, or in addition to, their security force.

IV   Creating Social Change

In Europe, at Glasgow's flagship museum, Kelvingrove Gallery and Museum, we find another traditional interdisciplinary museum dedicated to visitors—but this time, a unique social mission drives the institution. Glasgow's unusual city government places the arts on equal footing with health, education, and sports. Considering all of these to be fundamental amenities of social life, civic leaders act on the belief that art and culture should be available to all. We start with an admission-free museum that invites the community in to use its space as a commons.

While its mission was clear, the Kelvingrove team spent many years developing plans and raising funds for its visitor-centered reinvention. As we've seen elsewhere, the team also relied on strong and thoughtful leadership—a necessary component of managing the long road to change. In this case, Mark O'Neill paved the way with his own rich philosophy of social change. In response to the new mission, the museum also created cross-functional teams where, for example, curators report to research and curatorial managers, who have the institution's relation to its public foremost in mind.

In Kelvingrove's reinstallation, teams applied principles of community relevance to the display of art, history, and natural history collections. These varied displays were informed by visitor research—now a built-in component of their process. Focused on local interests, the new teams created collection exhibits that showcase community themes and prioritize visitors of all ages, including children. In a controversial decision, expert viewers were explicitly de-prioritized. These changes understandably provoked a range of reactions, from pleasure to outrage.

Taking its community mandate even further, Glasgow Museums created Nitshill Open Storage, a facility where every collection object not on display in the downtown museums is available for viewing.

In sync with its social mission, at Kelvingrove we see examples of all six visitor-centered themes: the importance of audience research, varied interpretive modes integrated in the galleries, community connection, a visitor-centered mission, strong leadership, and new forms of teamwork.

While still protecting the collections, Glasgow's museums have found a way to invert the priority most museums give to objects over people.

IV Creating Social Change

11 Kelvingrove

Museum as Cultural Commons

Kelvingrove Art Gallery and Museum in Glasgow, Scotland is a place where a young mum with kids, a retiree on a fixed income, or an unemployed laborer can spend the day for free, feasting their eyes on a Rembrandt, a Botticelli, or a grand gallery of Impressionist masterworks, not to mention an elephant and a dinosaur. The flagship institution of Culture and Sport Glasgow (a community interest company largely funded by the city), Kelvingrove is a sprawling red sandstone palace that is equal parts picture gallery, history museum, and natural history museum. It was conceived in the Victorian era and inaugurated at the 1901 International Exhibition—at the peak of the British Empire's wealth and influence, in what was at the time the empire's second largest city.

The museum holds a special place in the hearts of Glaswegians of all stripes: it is *their* museum, a common backdrop for their memories and life passages from childhood on. Even before the building's retrofit began in 2003, locals reported that they visited an average of six times a year—a statistic that would make museum leaders in other cities jealous. For some locals, the very thought of modifying the building or the gallery installations was anathema. "Don't ruin it!" was a common refrain in the community meetings that preceded the renovation. After a three-year, £28-million retrofit and gallery reinstallation, Kelvingrove reopened in 2006, surpassing all attendance expectations and briefly becoming the second most-visited museum in the entire United Kingdom.[1] The reinstallation had a polarizing effect. Some museum practitioners championed it. Museum consultant and author Elaine Heumann Gurian wrote:

> There are a few memorable paradigm-shifting museums that come along in any lifetime. I think of the United States Holocaust Memorial Museum; Te Papa: The National Museum of New Zealand; and the Guggenheim Bilbao. They are directed by chief executives who have vision and audacity. I add Kelvingrove to the list.[2]

Others went so far as to call for an inquisition and the placement of then-director Mark O'Neill's head on a spike—"symbolically speaking, of course."[3] What precisely elicited this particular crisis in the culture wars?

Figure 11.1 Kelvingrove Art Gallery and Museum in Kelvingrove Park, Glasgow.

With the long overdue renovation of the Victorian building and electrical system came a new interpretive approach as well; the art collections, which had previously been relegated to the rarely accessed second floor, were now distributed throughout the building on both floors. An extensive audience research campaign led to the decision to abandon the old presentation—objects organized according to Victorian taxonomies and divided by discipline—in favor of presenting the collections in a series of stories "rooted in history, but told from a contemporary perspective" to assure their relevance to today's varied publics.[4] "By using stories, we're trying to tap into the mythic psychology of fictional storytelling, but relating it to nonfictional histories of objects," said O'Neill, who led the transformation.[5]

Honoring Complex Truths: Using Startling Juxtapositions to Provoke New Insights

Encyclopedic museums have their virtues. At Kelvingrove, in place of the traditional "Arms and Armour" displays, we see the ingenious inventions humans have come up with to protect (and assault) in a dangerous world. Large glass cases present the following combinations:

- articulated sections of a suit of armor juxtaposed with a lobster and an armadillo;
- photos of a spraying beetle, a soldier aiming a machine gun, and a jet fighter united by the caption, "The further, faster, and more accurately you can throw an object, the more chance you have of winning";
- and the gaping jawbone of a great white shark transpierced by a swordfish blade, alongside an array of swords and spears.

The entire installation comes under the name Conflict and Consequence. Its subtitle is "How we keep inventing new ways of killing people, and then wonder why."

Figure 11.2 Kelvingrove: articulated armor meets its armadillo inspiration in *Conflict and Consequence* gallery.

Every story must have an audience—and Kelvingrove had many. Research and Curatorial Manager Martin Bellamy describes the variety of targets they were aiming to reach:

We had a set number of different audiences . . . it ranged from audiences with special needs—hearing or visual impairment; there were teenagers;

there was a family audience; and then there was a kind of catch-all, non-expert audience. There wasn't an audience for dedicated, knowledgeable professionals.

We didn't [have an expert audience] because basically, the core audience for Kelvingrove is very much a family audience. We do have a lot of professionals coming and having a look at and appreciating our paintings, but they basically know it all. They don't really need our help. It's the other audiences that need our help. And so that's where the meaningfulness of the interpretation lay.

Much of the criticism that has erupted since Kelvingrove's reopening implies that in their zeal to serve the disenfranchised, the museum may have overcompensated, leaving the established audience of educated (but non-specialist) museum-goers disgruntled, feeling abandoned.

Kelvingrove *is* a different kind of institution. It is operated by Culture and Sport Glasgow, also known simply as *Glasgow Life*—a public benefit charitable organization founded by the city's Labour government to run no less than thirteen museums, thirty-four community libraries, four national performing arts companies, fourteen leisure/sport centers, seven swimming pools, thirty-eight soccer fields (aka "football pitches"), and fourteen recreation centers for the residents of Glasgow and the city's visitors.

This community company's mission is "to inspire Glasgow's citizens and visitors to lead richer and more active lives through culture, sport and learning."[6] The museums, libraries, and football pitches are considered not merely cultural and recreational resources, but therapeutic forces, aiding community members of all backgrounds to overcome the setbacks of poverty, unemployment, substance abuse, and social isolation by giving them tools for leading more fulfilling and healthy lives. For even as Glasgow refashions itself as a modern, tech-savvy, service economy/tourist destination—having closed its last factories and mines many years ago and sand-blasted its once grimy façades—almost a third of its population still "experiences the greatest poverty and lowest level of educational attainment in Britain, and by some measures (such as heart disease) the worst health anywhere in the developed world."[7]

More germane to the subject of this book, Glasgow Life actively combats traditional stereotypes of art as "linked to education, income, and status—[as] 'not for the likes of us.'" It turns Bourdieu's argument that art and high culture are used as a differentiating factor between social elites and the masses right on its head, taking the masses as its target audience and, to hear some tell it, disenfranchising the so-called "cultured classes." The first tenet of its action plan is: Democratize High Culture.

The obligations of justice are not secondary to, or in competition with, what traditionally have been regarded as the core functions of museums: research, preservation, and display. Nor is the requirement to provide access—on a fair basis in terms of the realities of people's lives—inimical to the pursuit of values such as intellectual rigor and beauty. The objective is to create access to the truth and power of the objects for anyone who might be interested, regardless of their educational, economic, social or cultural background."[8]

Of course, it's one thing to maintain that the arts and culture are a therapeutic path capable of healing self-destructive behavior and anomie resulting from unemployment or broken families. It's another to figure out what that might mean in practice. The Kelvingrove reinstallation team was determined to begin. In the words of Mark O'Neill:

> We embarked on a vast program of engagement with visitors and non-visitors with the objective of removing the cultural, social, and psychological barriers to the museum as a whole and to the meanings of individual objects.[9]

The goals of the reinstall included making collections more physically and intellectually accessible to both new and traditional audiences. We can see the fruit of their front end research in their storytelling approach, aimed at developing threads that reach across collections. "Every object has dozens of attributes and dozens of aspects . . . we select the one that's most likely to trigger contemporary people's interests. Our mantra was 'The most interesting stories about the most interesting objects.'"[10] Those narratives don't shrink from difficult but relevant themes such as domestic violence or armed conflict, and they even address the compromised provenance of some museum objects—spoils gleaned from colonialism and conquest. O'Neill speaks of "resisting the temptation to celebrate human creativity at the expense of denial of the destructiveness of human nature."[11]

When Kelvingrove reopened, the public response to a gallery installation that included—but by no means emphasized—difficult subject matter was mixed, sometimes retracing the longstanding political schisms between the Labour and Conservative parties. Less politically progressive audiences objected to the "moralizing tone," which they associated with the ruling Labour City Council, though the greatest objections were reserved for what some visitors—in both high and low circles—perceived as a dumbing down of interpretive content. One commentator objected to the thematizing of all collections:

> The museum scripts the story, imposes the correct interpretation, and suggests the appropriate emotional response . . . The thematic approach is all well and good for special exhibitions, but when applied across the board the feeling is that visitors are being forced into participating in a scripted learning experience.[12]

He expressed nostalgia for the old Victorian-period galleries, that 19th-century imperium of knowledge—or semblance thereof. In some ways those taxonomic displays felt more open-ended to him than what he perceived as the heavy-handed didacticism of the new Kelvingrove.

> Whereas the museum used to be like a 3D filing cabinet from which one could draw material to back up a more general knowledge—or simply browse and wonder—the feeling now is altogether more curricular.

At Kelvingrove, exhibit labels clock in at thirty words. What's more, the interpretive strategy de-emphasizes the cult of celebrity around individual artists: in a twist unheard of in American museums, artist name comes *last* on the label, after the title and a brief text rooted in the object, including "why the object is important enough to be on display." "People just don't read big, dense labels," says curatorial manager Bellamy, who conducted front end research on the topic. "They read the first couple of sentences and then move on. So we thought, 'Okay, we'll just give them the first couple of sentences. We'll fit everything that we need in those first couple of sentences.'" He admits that this limit, mandated from above, was the single biggest bone of contention with the curators, but points out that with over 8,000 labeled objects on view, 30 words each still amounts to the length of a Dickens novel: 240,000 words.[13]

Kelvingrove staff also prioritized families as a central audience by including at least one story for children in every gallery, and hanging even important paintings at child height—in one case, a Picasso and a Dufy. In the Impressionist gallery, which staff knew from past experience was a favorite with visitors, they went so far as to place interactive art games on an island in the middle of the gallery to occupy kids so the parents could have a quiet moment strolling around the perimeter looking at their favorite works.

They also designed an entirely child-focused Mini-Museum on the ground floor, a sort of introductory sampler that focuses on faces and feet culled from throughout the collection. (Think about a child's eye view of most picture galleries!)

Figure 11.3a–b Kelvingrove: painting and object label. Note brevity of text and reversal of standard label hierarchy.

Figure 11.4 Kelvingrove: Raoul Dufy painting with story-based touchscreen interactive, both at child height.

Most people who have commented on Kelvingrove's reinstallation in online forums acknowledge the attention paid to the needs of children and families. But some feel that the more seasoned, adult audience that has been visiting the gallery faithfully since they themselves were children, has been slighted:

> There's nothing wrong with the idea that kids should be engaged by art. Hanging the paintings lower so children can see them properly with information aimed at their age group is sound thinking. When I heard this was the plan for Kelvingrove I applauded it.
>
> But then, I wrongly assumed that there would also be information panels for adults beside each work of art. If I like a piece I want to know all about it. I want to be challenged. I want to read something I perhaps don't fully understand which stretches me and compels me to investigate further. That is the basis of learning and it's part of the pleasure of art appreciation.
>
> It's ok though—it's not going to take another multi-million pound refurbishment to fix this—just put information panels for adults beside all the kids ones and we'll all be much happier![14]

This attention to one audience at the perceived expense of another seems at the heart of much of the controversy surrounding Kelvingrove—and other

Figure 11.5a–b Kelvingrove: touchscreen kiosk below John Pettie painting leads visitors through the heroine's suitor selection, with the terms of her choices updated to reflect contemporary Glasgow life.

visitor-centered museums. Coming upon an interactive kiosk set directly below a Victorian story painting by John Pettie, "aimed at teenagers and modeled on the quizzes found in girls' magazines,"[15] a group of adolescents might be thrilled. Others of a more traditional stripe might be appalled at the borrowing of conventions from tabloid journalism and comic books, not to mention the gleeful laughter of the teens.[16]

Open Museum, Open Storage

Reinventing museums such as Kelvingrove that are already destinations and offering them to the public free of charge is only one aspect of Glasgow Museums' remit. Two other complementary and innovative strategies presaged the Kelvingrove reinstall and extend its public vocation in unprecedented ways. First, as far back as 1990, before the words "diversity" and "inclusion" entered the vocabulary of mainstream museum practice, Glasgow had pioneered The Open Museum, an outreach program whose mandate was to "facilitate free access to the collections to those who don't, won't, or can't visit the museum." Readers might question the notion that museums are accountable for both the publics they reach and the publics they don't, but Glasgow Museums' leaders felt strongly that responsibility for sharing the benefits of culture did not stop at their door. Mark O'Neill speaks of populations that write museums off:

> It is because of a sense that museums are not for them. This may be due to a whole range of factors, from transport availability and cost, to outdated perceptions of what museums are like. It may also be a lack of confidence, which is experienced as a fear of embarrassment for not knowing the rules, a sense of being unfamiliar with the rituals and etiquette of museum visiting. Above all it is an anticipation of not being made welcome, by staff who will detect their inexperience, and by other visitors, who will resent the presence of outsiders.[17]

When we hear American museum directors speak of their own trustees lingering in the lobby waiting to be escorted into the galleries rather than venturing forth by themselves, is it any wonder that people from marginalized communities feel intimidated about entering a museum?

With these audiences in mind, the Open Museum was founded. The guiding concept was to work with members of various sub-communities within the city to curate small, trunk-sized, portable mini-exhibitions and "reminiscence kits" that could travel to neighborhoods and be shown or shared in libraries, community and leisure centers, retirement homes—even prisons. Whenever possible, actual collection objects would be used rather than replicas or pieces from "study collections."

> The Open Museum is dedicated to widening ownership of the city's collection. It aims to free the reserves, which lie hidden in the stores and

cupboards, and to forge a link between the skills of our staff and the needs of interested groups. Above all we want to create a museum which is related to the lives of the people in their own communities.[18]

The themes for these shows vary widely, as dictated by the interests of the community partners in dialogue with the collection curators. Topics range from Football to Shipbuilding, from Fifties Music to Stone Age Technology, passing through Insects, Shopping, Childcare, and Tenement Life along the way. As the process has gained momentum, the exhibits "rapidly changed from being very museum-focused to being much more obviously community-led with more emphasis on contemporary issues." Kits or exhibits were developed about the breast vs. bottle debate, domestic violence, homelessness, the veil in Islam, gay relationships, and ethnic groups present in the Glasgow population from the Poles to the Sikhs. Any topic about which one community has specialized knowledge that could be shared with others is fair game. Curators and designers are tasked with working with at least one outside group, and putting themselves at the service of that group's interests rather than dictating the topic or final object selection.

The intention was to deliver what people wanted rather than what the museum thought they wanted or what the museum thought they ought to want.

The Open Museum was first piloted in 1990. By 2000, there were some 884 exhibitions and kits reaching almost 400,000 people a year. Tangible impacts included:

- Enhancing the sense of self-respect and empowerment for people who normally felt left behind, at the fringes of society
- Taking dozing dementia patients in elder care facilities out of their stupor and snapping them vividly back to life as they handled clothing, tools, toys, washing kits, and memorabilia from their youth
- Raising morale and sense of self-respect in the face of the diminishments of age
- Blurring the boundaries between museums and the libraries that often presented these exhibits, at a time when libraries were seeking to redefine their own community service role
- Engaging other community institutions as exhibition locales, including old age homes, civic buildings, sport facilities, airports
- Changing participating community members' notion of the museum itself, e.g., "Museums are not as stuffy as they used to be when . . . it was just a glass case with a stuffed animal behind it and that was an animal—that was it and sshhh—don't speak. It is fun now and an experience."[19]

Such success could have simply led to an expansion of the outreach program, leaving the museums themselves untouched. Instead, the 1999–2000 annual review performed by the Glasgow Museums leadership recommended that "the entire museum service take on its philosophy." And so it was that the involvement of community groups became a guiding principle in the reinstallation of Kelvingrove that began in 2003 and in the stories that were highlighted in its interpretive plan.

Another consequence was that the museums' collection storage facility, which prior to renovation had been housed in Kelvingrove's musty and over-cluttered basement, was moved to a spanking new collection care and research center at the edge of town, the Glasgow Museums Resource Centre in Nitshill. Every object that is not on view in the thirteen city museums is available for public viewing and study here. Says Martin Bellamy: "The fundamental concept is that the collections belong to the people of Glasgow. Therefore, they have every right to consult at Nitshill."

You enter this million-object repository to find orientation rooms, classrooms, study rooms, and storage "pods." Each "pod" in storage has itself been curated: objects of greatest interest are nearest the doors, arrayed on racks, shelving, or the floor, depending on footprint and size. (On the floor of some storage rooms, old trolley cars, hulking medical machinery of yesteryear, and omnibuses!) In the art storage pods—each climate-controlled to suit its particular medium—sliding racks group landscapes, still lifes, or paintings from a specific period: so many teachable moments. Worlds of major and minor arcana unfold before your eyes as you move from room to room. Nitshill has a full daily program of public visitation—as busy as many a downtown museum. Bellamy recounts:

> There are school groups that go around in the morning. And then you can turn up at half past two and go right on a [storage] tour. At the beginning, we just had kind of general tours . . . but now we're doing a range of specialist tours, where the curators of different subjects will do a tour of natural history or art or technology. Every day.

Open Storage at Nitshill

Figure 11.6a–b Glasgow Museums Resource Centre, Nitshill: open storage with painting racks arranged by theme; early communications technology.

Figure 11.6c–d 1910 butcher's van; Rolls-Royce test engine for the Concorde supersonic plane.

Figure 11.7 Glasgow Museums Resource Centre: school kids on field trip.

> "The fundamental concept is that the collections belong to the people of Glasgow. Therefore, they have every right to consult at Nitshill."
> —Martin Bellamy, Research & Curatorial Manager

At Kelvingrove, volunteer docents give the gallery tours. But because the specialists have their offices in the collections storage facility at the edge of town, Nitshill offers a curatorial tour through the store rooms at 2:45, seven days a week. We know of no other museum that offers such extensive public service.

There is grist here for hundreds of school groups a year, and it's not just for schools; by official Glasgow Museums policy and given sufficient notice, anyone—expert or layperson—can come here to see any object from their museums' collections. According to Bellamy:

It's a range of visiting academics, professors from foreign universities looking at something very particular, to people whose family had donated stuff to the museum and they're doing their own family research and they want to see something in the collection. Just basic curiosity.

The staff is literally at the public's service. In fact, the Glasgow Museums take this mandate for public access one step further. Nitshill has also become the repository for all of the Open Museum's portable exhibit/reminiscence kits—now seventy in number. The kits are loaned out over a thousand times a year and are seen by an estimated 24,000 people.[20]

So if you want to visit the red Victorian palace of Kelvingrove—there is, after all, a free daily concert on their massive pipe organ, illustrious centerpiece of the main hall at 1:00 p.m.—or take your schoolkids on a field trip to Nitshill to view curated open storage and make their own mini-exhibitions of toys from past eras in a classroom on-site, or if you want to bring a museum exhibit back to your neighborhood, hobby group, retirement home, or even prison, the Glasgow Museums want you to know that their collection is not theirs at all. They are merely the guardians, scholars, collection managers, and caretakers. If you are a Glaswegian, "their" collection is yours.

Key Takeaways

1. Glasgow's museums have a history of putting collections in service to citizens. The city government holds that the arts are a fundamental need and amenity of social life, and should be free to the public.
2. Kelvingrove's cross-functional teams apply principles of community relevance to the display of art, history, and natural history collections. Object labels clock in at 30–50 words, and every object on view has one.

3. Glasgow Museums Research Center at Nitshill takes the commitment to community a step higher yet. Making every object universally available while still protecting the collection is a bold initiative, worthy of a committed public institution.

Notes

1 After the pent-up demand of the 2007 year brought 2.2 million visitors, attendance has dropped back down to more predictable historic averages.
2 Elaine Heumann Gurian. "Exhibitions: Kelvingrove Art Gallery and Museum, Glasgow, Scotland." *Curator: The Museum Journal* 50, 3 (2007): 358–361.
3 Stephen Dawber. "Blairism on the Walls at Kelvingrove." *Variant* 27. http://www.variant.org.uk/27texts/kelvingrove27.html Accessed August 26, 2014.
4 Fiona McLeod (Ed.). *Essential Kelvingrove*. London: Glasgow Museums Publishing in association with Philip Wilson Publishers, 2010, p. 24.
5 He is now Director of Policy and Research for Glasgow Life.
6 Glasgow Life. Glasgow Life Vision Statement. http://www.glasgowlife.org.uk/about-us/Pages/Glasgow-Life-Vision-Statement.aspx Accessed July 20, 2015.
7 Mark O'Neill. "Kelvingrove: Telling Stories in a Treasured Old/New Museum." *Curator: The Museum Journal* 50, 4 (October 2007): 381.
8 Ibid., 395.
9 Ibid., 386.
10 O'Neill quoted in Jeanne M. Liedtka and Randy Salzman. "Leading Innovation at Kelvingrove." J. Paul Getty Trust and University of Virginia Darden School Foundation, 2009. http://ssrn.com/abstract=1584555
11 O'Neill. (2007): 395.
12 Gordon MacGregor. "Benighted at the Museum." *Scottish Review*. http://www.scottishreview.net/GMacGregor212.html Accessed August 28, 2014.
13 *Great Expectations,* for example, clocks in at 183,349 words; to cite an American example, *Moby Dick* hits 206,052.
14 Post by Liam Baxter to Glasgow online forum. http://discuss.glasgowguide.co.uk/lofiversion/index.php/t20239.html Accessed August 31, 2014.
15 Sue Latimer. "Art for Whose Sake?" In Juliette Fritsch (Ed.), *Museum Gallery Interpretation and Material Culture*. London: Routledge, 2011, p. 72.
16 It turns out this kiosk and another in the gallery, both developed in collaboration with members of their targeted age groups, are engaging people in closer consideration of paintings they might otherwise walk by, but they are the closest juxtaposition of a luminous touchscreen—and an irreverent interactive—to a painting these authors have ever seen.
17 Mark O'Neill. "Preface." In the Research Centre for Museums and Galleries in the Department of Museum Studies at the University of Leicester, *A Catalyst for Change: The Social Impact of the Open Museum*. Leicester: Research Centre for Museums and Galleries, University of Leicester, 2002, p. 2.
18 Ibid., p. 8.
19 Results paraphrased from *Catalyst*; quote ibid., p. 25.
20 Martin Bellamy. Personal communication.

V Taking a Critical Stance on Museum Practice

At the Van Abbe Museum and the Museum of Contemporary Art in Denver (MCA Denver) we find a different, often experimental approach to visitor engagement. Here, energetic leaders, while engaging audiences in new ways, also take a critical stance toward museums as public institutions. Both museums use social practice as a tool to engage visitors in "the life of art." Whether through live events (MCA Denver) or through radical in-gallery interpretive approaches or games (Van Abbe), their leaders see the museum's job as one of critical engagement, with or without the use of traditional museum collections/objects.

At Van Abbe, Director Charles Esche wants to turn the museum into a tool for imagining the world differently and more critically. Using in-house expertise, he invites community in by asking visitors to participate with challenging ideas and approaches.

This model of museum practice prioritizes contemporary perspectives over historic collections—going so far as to question canonical works. Esche's notions of *radical hospitality* and visitor participation also extend to changed organizational structures, even as he seeks to ensure collegiality among staff as they take on new roles.

MCA Denver, free of a permanent collection, focuses on live programming and real-time community interaction. Led by Adam Lerner, an experienced and inspired Millennial, they reinvent organizational structures by purposefully hiring for the individual rather than the role. The prevailing work ethos values creativity over title and position.

Both museums might be considered creative workshops where new ideas grow and visitors and museum professionals alike are challenged by fresh approaches. These museums also offer a window into the future, leading us to consider not only new forms of visitor engagement, but also changing definitions of the museum itself.

12 Van Abbe Museum
Radicality Meets Hospitality

The Van Abbe takes everything we've seen so far and inflects it in a new direction: Director Charles Esche is intent on using contemporary art practice as a way of opening both museum exhibitions and visitor roles to greater transparency.

The museum's watchword of *radical hospitality* embodies an attitude that doesn't shrink from asking provocative questions, but says "we'll go there with you and puzzle it out together." Questioning extends to the collections themselves; beginning in a two-year series of shows titled *Play Van Abbe*, Esche undermined the time-honored "museum as treasure house" mode of presentation. He invited contemporary artists to critique or extend the utopian premises of earlier artists by interacting with their works. These dialogues lay bare the vagaries of artistic creation, art history, the art market, and museum canon formation.

Such efforts at critical reflection have extended to back-of-house museum functions as well. In the effort to break down entrenched silos and make the staff itself more collaborative, Esche instituted new team processes, reshuffled reporting structures, and created a new position—Experience Designer— whose job is to bridge the gulf between traditional curatorial and education roles in a way that is both clever about the art and attuned to the visitors.

•

"I have, at the heart of it, a particular desire to see if, through art, we can imagine the world otherwise."
—Van Abbe Director Charles Esche

Charles Esche, the British-born director of the Van Abbe Museum in Eindhoven, Holland, takes a radical stance: he is against the museum as treasure house. His is a vision of the activist museum: a toolset for critical inquiry rather than a chapel for the reverent worship of objects.

In a sense, the currency of a museum is the imagination, rather than money . . . So it doesn't promote just an affirmation of bourgeois taste or the status quo or of existing traditions, but actually promotes . . . critical reflection about those conditions and how they might be *otherwise*.

How, we might ask, does a museum avoid the trap of giving in to the legacy of past generations—paying homage before an array of sanctified treasures—and instead provoke visitors to think and act in new ways? In Esche's estimation, most museums don't even try.

If art museums aim to preserve examples of rule-breaking and paradigm-shifting behavior for future generations, why, one might ask, are their atmospheres so hushed and reverent? How can you maintain the radicalism of some legacy artworks in a way that is relevant and sensate to viewers today without first turning those visitors into art historians?

Esche cites his countryman T. J. Clark, who on the cusp of the 21st century, wrote: "Modernity is our antiquity . . . The forms of representation it originally gave rise to are unreadable." In this light, modern art is already disconnected from the lives of people today. Picasso may as well belong to antiquity; the same with Matisse—even Pollock. How do we make these works *readable*, in all their radicality, in today's terms?

> My hopes were that . . . the collection would be, in a sense, revolutionized, in terms of turned upside-down; and that . . . the works in the collection would once again return some of their modernist alienation.

Esche is aware of the failure of contemporary audiences to connect with many artworks and he has a theory as to why they don't. We have a disjunction, characterized by viewers saying or even thinking, "I don't understand." Esche suggests:

> "I don't understand" is a displaced way of saying "I don't think it's very good," but not wanting to say so in case it *is* good and they've got it wrong.[1]

On the other hand, how would they know or judge if something *is* good? As Esche observes elsewhere: "Modern art . . . requires of its makers that they re-invent themselves and their definitions with every new piece of art that is made."[2] With such shifting sands, we might well ask how a viewer is supposed to keep up. Is it enough to simply trust the museum's authority? Such a position disempowers the visitor—the exact opposite of Esche's goal.

As a result, the Van Abbe has been experimenting with new ways of connecting with their visitors. In fact, they've turned themselves into a lab of sorts, developing a plethora of new tools and approaches geared to making their museum and the artworks it contains feel as participatory and strange as contemporary life. In so doing, they raise the bar—for their visitors, their staff, and their artworks.

"Start with the visitor's world and understand that every artwork can be contextualized in a way that relates to contemporary life in society."

That's Hadas Zemer Ben-Ari, reiterating a leitmotif of this book. Zemer is an Israeli designer who first arrived at the Van Abbe as an intern from the Netherlands Design Institute and went on to be named the museum's first official "Experience Designer." Motivated by a transformative agenda and a sometimes challenging collection, the Van Abbe has taken a stance they dub *Radical Hospitality*. How does it work in practice? The role of dialogue—or exchange, as Zemer calls it—is central, "because you'd like to include the other on your journey."

•

Situated as it is in a small city in Holland, the Van Abbe may seem an unlikely place to find the largest collection outside of Moscow of artworks by El Lissitzky. Lissitzky was a Russian constructivist who flourished in the early decades of the twentieth century. His are among the first generation of non-objective works: flat red and black squares set at an angle and intersected by dynamic lines of force—vectors of progress, or so the artist believed.

Lissitzky's work at the Van Abbe is spread across a handful of galleries. In its effort to restore the urgency to these objects, the curator collaborated with an educator/communications specialist. Together, they developed an exhibition that both respects the artworks and provides deep and varied contextual reference material. Among their approaches:

- commissioning human-scaled sculptures that bring the artist's abstract drawings to life (Figure 12.1)
- embedding monitors in the gallery walls to display looping slideshows and archival film clips of Russian avant-garde artist collectives and performances
- presenting floor-to-ceiling display cases filled with archival posters and documentation (Figure 12.2)
- fabricating large gallery-scaled mock-ups of Lissitzky's utopian architectural projects (e.g., horizontal skyscrapers)
- projecting Russian avant-garde filmmaker Dziga Vertov's classic experimental work, *Man with a Movie Camera*
- and, finally, punctuating the exhibition with quotes from Lissitzky demonstrating his revolutionary idealism—with the type set at an angle in a modern, sans serif font

All in all, you could call this an interpretive full court press: a carefully orchestrated effort to plunge the visitor back into the mindset of Lissitzky and his peers in their visionary moment.

Into this completed exhibition, director Esche introduced a subversive agent.

As we visit these galleries, every so often we notice small, handwritten words crawling along like insects atop the pristine typography, undermining

Figure 12.1 Van Abbe Museum: 3-D sculpture made in 2009 after El Lissitzky's *New Man*, 1923 (as interpreted by Prof. John Milner and produced by Henry Milner, 2009).

Figure 12.2 Van Abbe Museum: El Lissitzky galleries with display cases for ephemera on left and computer-based slide show inset in wall.

the authority of the installation. They are the work of a contemporary Bulgarian artist, Nedko Solakov. Under Stalin, Lissitzky's utopian dream of revolution turned into a nightmare—and for generations to come, hundreds of millions of people, among them Bulgarians, were on the receiving end of the failed promise of the Soviet Empire. When Esche invited Solakov to look at Lissitzky's utopian vision through the prism of his (Solakov's) experience, the artist did so derisively.

Narrative and counter-narrative travel side-by-side on these walls: Russian utopian idealism countered by post-Soviet cynicism. Together, they offer a more complex view.

The graffiti on the walls renders the whole exhibit more accessible. These esoteric paintings are once again fresh and controversial. They're re-endowed with idealism, if only because they're being called out as false. A deception. The gloves are off. Art matters and we're going to fight about it, even if

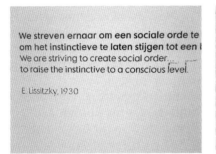 

Figure 12.3a–b Van Abbe Museum: El Lissitzky quote with Nedko Solakov commentary.

Figure 12.4 Van Abbe Museum: another Lissitzky quote with Solakov repartee: "A GOD is playing with/a constructivist puzzle/desperately trying to create a black Square."

the debate starts with a voice as small as an ant. By definition, everything in museums is special, but here it's not sacrosanct. It's been opened up for critical reflection. The air has been let back into the room.

In so doing, the Van Abbe is violating what may be the first law of Modernist museology: Each artist gets his or her own little acre, his or her cubit of space. Typically, each artist's truth is permitted to reign as absolute within the four walls of their gallery—if they are fortunate enough to receive a whole gallery—or, as is more often the case, within the four to eight linear feet of their wall allocation. No one else gets to break into that space except the curator, who normally upholds the artist's truth.

In this sense, most modern art museums can be seen as spaces of multiple paths to truth, or even conflicting propositions about reality. Each artist gets space to place his or her competitive bid for salvation, uncontested. By inviting Solakov's subversive overlay of a counter-narrative, the museum reveals the glory and Achilles heel of every modern artist: that their modes of expression are nothing but subjective responses, each one vying for an audience.

In doing so, the museum also opens up a dialogue—an exchange with its viewers—for they, too, it turns out, have powers of agency, arriving with their own life experience and forms of authority. It is with this in mind that the Van Abbe began inviting visitors to actively tag the artworks in its galleries. They developed the Live Encounter Tagging System (LETS), a far more open-ended variant of the exhibit label. Starting with galvanized metal plates, they placed object ID info across the bottom and left the remainder for tags contributed by the curators ("static tags") and the public ("interactive tags").

Figure 12.5a–b Van Abbe Museum: object labels with space above for tags contributed by curators and visitors.

The goal was to turn each label into a suggestive exchange. Understandably, there was some reluctance on the part of many visitors—especially older ones—to commit themselves in quite so public a manner. That was where the Van Abbe's volunteer Museum Hosts kicked in, serving as "tag pushers." The hosts actively recruited viewers, and found in the open label space a perfect icebreaker. Zemer explains:

> What the tags did was to supply a practical reason for opening a conversation—explaining the appearance of the peculiar metal plates and words in the exhibition halls; from there it was much easier to continue discussing art, interpretations and meanings.[3]

As old tags were removed to make room for new ones, the words were input into a database for future reference.

As an integral part of the 2009–2011 experimental reinstallations titled *Play Van Abbe*, the museum called attention to the roles visitors adopt (consciously or un-), and subjected them to the same meta-level scrutiny. In *Play Van Abbe 4*, as visitors entered the museum, the Museum Hosts—now dubbed "Game Masters"—invited them to adopt one of three roles:

- the *Pilgrim*, whose attitude before the collection is one of wonder, perhaps enhanced by a hungry mind desirous of learning more about the works on display;
- the *Tourist*, who is on a mission to see the most important works in the collection, to catch the highlights tour;
- the *Flaneur*, always on the lookout for a serendipitous encounter, be it with a person, an artwork, or their environment as a whole.

With each persona came a prop—a tool to aid the visitors in their role:

- for the *Pilgrim*, a traditional audio tour, offering interpretive background regarding the artworks;
- for the *Tourist*, a somewhat fantastical map, tracing an itinerary to the highlights;
- for the *Flâneur*, two props: an audio soundscape—fluid, without stops or commentary—and a journal in which to record their observations and impressions.[4]

Furthermore, different artworks had been pre-selected as most apt to interest each persona; the initials of the personas (*P*, *T*, or *F*) were prominently displayed on object labels so as to attract their target audience from across a gallery. If they so desired, visitors were allowed to shift from one persona to another at a station midway through the museum, swapping out their props in the process—but few did.

Of course, one might well ask: do most people go to a museum to be challenged or to be reassured? For some, this double undermining—both of time-tested artworks and of visitors' viewing habits—might prove more stressful than freeing. This is where hospitality comes in: the warmth of human presence. In *Play Van Abbe 4*, at the end of their museum visit, visitors were invited to convene again with a Game Master—this time to chart and reflect on their itinerary through the museum. The dialogue took place around a digital touchtable displaying a map of the museum's galleries. Salient artworks could be flagged as they talked; at the end, a souvenir map of their unique visit was printed and delivered to them. Some cognitive loops were closed, others opened, but for those who chose to participate, the art had been made real for that day with the added impetus of an intelligent human interaction, aided by a technological support. Indeed, if the Game Master felt the visitor had reached a level of critical awareness about the art and their relation to it, s/he could give their interviewee a bonus "letter" as a kind of persona prize: W for Worker, certifying that this visitor had "worked" the museum, and had let the museum have an effect on them, too.[5]

This degree of critical reflection was exactly what Director Esche asked of himself and his staff. He talks about how the two-year sequence of *Play Van Abbe* exhibitions was conceived both to reconsider the museum's permanent collection and to reinvent the staff's way of working together.

Figure 12.6 Van Abbe Museum: Game Master with visitor using the Journey Recorder table in *Play Van Abbe 4: The Pilgrim, the Tourist, the Flaneur (and the Worker)*.

Before *Play,* there was very much the idea that curators were kind of islands of expertise somehow, that worked on their own projects and delivered their own exhibition. And I think after *Play,* that's not true anymore. . . . So once you wrap everything into one package and then you say, We're all part of this, then the question of ownership is, Okay, we all own this. So we can start to act like that. . . . It's the thing that really makes it enjoyable to work here, is the fact that we can work together.

Esche, who's the first to protest that he's not a born manager, nonetheless suggests that part of the success was due to the revised organizational charts he put out, provisional as they may have been:

Those charts were really important, so that people felt they knew where they fit in and what their role was and things like that. It never worked like that. [laughs] Never really bore much relationship to how it actually worked. But it was very important to have it . . . as an orientation device. The more security you can give, the more capacity for change people have, actually.

Chief Curator Christiane Berndes, an eighteen-year Van Abbe veteran, talks about the difference made by Esche's commitment to meta-thinking about organizational behavior:

Is it possible to do the job and at the same time rethink your job? Yes . . . without losing your motivation to do it.

We have this freedom here in the house, to experiment and to make mistakes, and to learn from our mistakes.

. . . You have to go to this meta level, at certain moments. And it's not easy. We don't do it that often, but we do it. We switch to the meta and say, What are we doing now?[6]

Key Takeaways

1. The Van Abbe uses contemporary art practice as a way of opening both museum exhibitions and visitor roles to a more critical view. The museum doesn't shrink from asking challenging questions, but embraces an attitude of radical hospitality.
2. Esche rejects the "museum as treasure house" model of presentation. He even goes so far as to invite contemporary artists to make visual critiques on the walls of the galleries.
3. In the effort to break down silos and make the staff itself more collaborative, Esche has instituted new team processes, reshuffled reporting structures, and created a new position to bridge the gulf between traditional curatorial and education roles.

Notes

1 Charles Esche and De Appel CP. "Stand I Don't." In Paul O'Neill and Mick Wilson (Eds.), *Curating and the Educational Turn*. London and Amsterdam: Open Editions and de Appel, 2010, pp. 297–309

2 Esche. "Start with a Table. . ." In Paul O'Neill and Mick Wilson (Eds.), *Curating and the Educational Turn*. London and Amsterdam: Open Editions and de Appel, 2010, pp. 310–319.

3 Hadas Zemer Ben-Ari. "Live Encounter Tagging System/A Test Case Review." In Yoeri Meessen and Thea Unteregger (Eds.), *Workbook: An Art Mediation Resource*. Amsterdam, The Netherlands: Manifesta, nd, 1–6. http://www.manifestaworkbook.org/Liveencounter.pdf Accessed June 8, 2015.

4 Compare these personas, or identities, to John Falk's entrance narratives for *Explorers*, who want to learn as much as they can about the objects on view; *Experience Seekers*, who are intent on checking all the "must-sees" off their list; and *Rechargers*, who seek little interpretive assistance but aspire to take a break from the hectic pace of the outside world.

5 Of course, it's still the museum representative, not the visitor, who gets to decide.

6 Here Berndes echoes Lisa Dent, former curator of contemporary art at Columbus, who, when asked for lessons to share with colleagues in the field, said: "Sitting around the table with educators and curators together, it's hard to imagine doing it a different way now. And I think it would be to remind myself again to never assume. I mean, just the assumptions I make about what people are interested in and what people will look at. It's just you're always learning."

13 Museum of Contemporary Art Denver

Experience over Objects

At MCA Denver they are reinventing in-house organizational structures to make innovation happen. In this environment, inspiration and creativity are valued over title and position. Here we find a youthful leader, Adam Lerner, who has also worked in more traditional art museums but now questions the very notion of museums.

Focused on social practice and live programming, the MCA's biggest gauge of success may simply be loyal attendance and the buzz of positive social media. With no permanent collection to worry about, Lerner and staff have the freedom and agility to experiment with both exhibitions and programming. Their challenge is to tie the events, which on the surface might simply look like entertainment, to underlying art ideas.

Lerner works in equal measure on developing his museum as a brand and on inspiring his team. Not confined to narrowly prescribed roles, staff members feel free to generate new ideas in the confidence that they will be heard. For visitors and staff alike, the museum environment is very much alive.

•

MCA Denver is a next-generation institution, led by one Gen-Xer and one Millennial; it is not riven by the often polarizing conflicts that have characterized the Boomers and their predecessors. It was born collection-free, without the pre-existing departments, structures, weights, and obligations of most other museums we have discussed. In that sense, it can be seen as both a parallel and a counterpoint to the City Museum in St. Louis. If City Museum's emphasis is on physical play and exploration of a multi-storied building steeped in St. Louis's past, the MCA Denver's is on conceptual play and performance in the fields of culture—high, low, and in between.

Neither City nor MCA Denver devotes a significant portion of its resources to the archival preservation and display of collections, or for that matter even focuses much on galleries per se. Instead, each offers its own form of improvisational exploration. And each has (or in one case, had) charismatic leaders defining its personality: at City Museum, the intensely hands-on Bob Cassilly; at MCA Denver, the conceptual artists of social aesthetics, less physical but equally irreverent and free-spirited, Adam Lerner and his partner in crime, Sarah Baie.

One way to begin to abolish silos and traditional thinking is to lose the nomenclature that creates them. Lerner's self-created title is "Director and Chief Animator, Department of Fabrications," while Baie's is "Chief of Fictions." If you look at the organizational chart, there are no curators or educators as such on staff. Lerner and Baie learned to avoid creating such polarizing dichotomies in the first place. They met while working in the Education Department at the Denver Art Museum, and what they saw there—in an institution that has been held up to the field as a model of curator-educator cooperation—was enough to make them decide they wanted to try something on their own. When they got the chance to invent their own organizational structure, they went another way altogether.

So what was it Lerner and Baie wanted to do differently? What was their new approach?

> We were very aware of the tiny silos that traditional museums fall in, where you have an education department and a curatorial department, and they often do not work well together. And we wanted to create a place where there weren't those kinds of silos . . .
>
> In not making a distinction between curatorial and education that's deeply substantive . . . we also are trying to connect this formal, traditional idea of art that's related to the history of the people in the past who we've called artists, to the broad range of creativity that's actually taking place in our culture today.

They take a little from each pot, and the fact that they don't have to defend an inherited collection means that they are unencumbered by the weight of history, the selections of prior curators, or, for that matter, by any restrictive definition of "art" itself.

In fact, the MCA's flagship program, *Mixed Taste*, has nothing to do with visual art per se. It is instead a series of public talks that goes back to Lerner and Baie's prior collaboration in The Lab at Belmar, an art space in an upscale suburban Denver mall that from 2004–2008 became something of a cult destination. Over their five years there, they developed quite a following, so much so that when MCA Denver was seeking a new director for its handsome new modernist home (a burnished steel and smoked glass showplace designed by the Tanzanian-British architect David Adjaye and built under the prior director, Cydney Payton) their board was persuaded to look to Lerner—a creative programmer rather than a curator/connoisseur of objects—to ensure the institution's vitality and relevance to the local audience.

Mixed Taste was a lecture series with a twist.

> The rules are simple: The first speaker speaks for a half-hour, then the next speaker speaks on a completely unrelated topic for a half-hour, and

then there is question and answer on both at the same time. During the first part of the program, speakers are not allowed to make connections between topics, during the question and answer, anything can happen.[1]

So the very structure of the talks guaranteed a) surprise, b) irreverence, and c) out-of-the-box thinking. No longer could any participant assume the mantle of Unquestioned Authority, coughing in his tweeds when someone asked him (or her) an impertinent question. The very leap of faith on which these talks were premised was that there was more to be learned at the edges of far-flung fields than at their centers . . . that the really interesting questions came from outsiders and from tangential points of view. A little knowledge might go far, but additional deep probes might jostle your fixed ideas and trigger new connections, especially when multiplied by all the people in the room brewing and digesting both topics at once.

Exemplary Topics

- Wittgenstein & Hula Dancing
- Susan Sontag & Paint by Numbers
- Bananas Foster & Emily Dickinson
- Raw Milk Cheese & Minimalist Art
- Marxism & Kittens, Kittens, Kittens

The result has been an ongoing dialogue between high and low culture—in Lerner's words, "to make culture feel enough like a joke, that it comes back around somehow and feels meaningful and important again."[2] (Think of the Van Abbe's effort to shock two vocabularies together—one of early abstraction, the other of comics and graffiti—both born in visual culture.)

So how is this a museum and not a performance space? Events and gatherings that cultivate the community's imagination are the creative currency in which MCA Denver now trades. Because the events the museum produces are immediate, live, and engaging, they typically don't need an interpretive layer. They carry their interpretation with them in the enthusiasm of shared public experience. As Lerner puts it,

> I actually think that these hybrid forms—which is really what we're going for—between education and curatorial and fun—I just think that those are what really interest us. The one thing I think that makes us very, very different from any institution, I've never seen another museum be self-effacing or have, like, humor. Another art museum, especially.

"Most museums," he says, "make a distinction between the events they produce and the art they display." He points out that they have a creative side, but keep it well hidden. It lives in their family programs or their fundraisers, both of which promise extraordinary experiences in the interest of enticing

a) parents to bring their kids or b) patrons to donate money. Meanwhile, back in the galleries, a silent sobriety reigns. In fact, he notes, curators often cringe when they see the liberties marketers or fundraisers take in the interest of driving traffic to the museum or raising money for its functions. Lerner feels this cognitive disconnect is psychologically damaging and prevents those institutions from speaking with a unified voice or making use of their creativity.

"Our audience," says Baie, "can't tell the difference, we've discovered, between a development event and a programming event. So why make such a fuss about it?"

MCA Denver's galleries may not be so different, but its Board and mission are:

> [There is] a much deeper throughline that the board has created, which is that what really matters is this: human connections. They're not a board that says, "We care most about how we can contribute to the discipline of art history or the field of contemporary art." We say that, "Yes, we want to make sure that we are, as an organization, exploring what art means to us as people. And you can do that any way you want."

Another big difference between the MCA and its more stodgy brethren—"normal" museum directors and curators—is that MCA leaders and staff feel empowered to play and to act as creative agents in their own right. Like the Van Abbe's recasting of its collection, the MNHS's Dan Spock's observation that "all museum-going is a form of play, and if you're in harmony with that as a museum-maker, then people appreciate it a great deal," and Bob Cassilly's ten-story immersive playground, the MCA revels in the play spirit. Reflecting back on her prior experience on museum education teams, Baie says: "We'd brainstorm to the point where people were laughing, and then we'd say: 'All right, dial it back.'" At the MCA, that self-imposed creative censure no longer applies. In fact, as Lerner's friend Nina Simon notes: "Adam and his colleagues are more like a conceptual art collective than arts administrators." Lerner and Baie encourage team members to propose programs: "We're small enough and the people work closely enough and they trust each other . . . We create a culture, and I let that culture be a producer."

So the museum's primary emphasis is neither on artists per se nor on objects. They do not relegate themselves to a supporting role for capital-A *Artists*: the culture heroes. Unlike leadership at institutions that focus on collection-building, MCA Trustees don't prioritize being the first to identify and invest in the next trending artists on the global art scene. And while most museums—even of contemporary art—define their role as arbiters of quality, preservers of treasures, and purveyors of definitive information, Lerner and Baie have publicly presented paintings of fictive provenance—e.g., in an exhibition they called *Unauthenticated Paintings of the Russian*

Avant-Garde—and produced live art events that included butchering bison and shearing sheep.

> Is that art? No, it's not art. I think it's actually more interesting than art. It touches the spirit of art, of why we even have art.

Out of their approximately 50,000 annual visitors, 10% come for the live events. They see the museum as a resource for new and creative forms of thinking and acting in community, expressed in real time. That said, Lerner and Baie both are quick to point out that theirs is not an "anything goes" situation.

> One lesson we learned very early on was that content is incredibly important to our audience. If we just have a party, it's not—We don't get the same kind of energy.

So the association with art and a practice rooted in aesthetics are essential; they're a sort of irreducible litmus test that draws their community in and makes them all feel smarter.

Lerner is cognizant of how different this approach is from that of his so-called peers:

> Most contemporary art museums . . . they still want to be somewhat audience-oriented, but they're basically never going to be to the right of center on audience-orientation. Never. We joke, like the ideal art exhibition is *Andy Warhol: The Impressionist Years*. But it's really hard to get anything audience-oriented for a contemporary art museum.

He sees the older generation of museum professionals, educated in the 1960s and 1970s, as still caught in a conflict between Authority and Democracy, the former embodied by the curators, the latter by the educators. The younger generation is less caught up by old polarities or the siloed institutional structures that perpetuated them.

> They don't see themselves as in a conflict. What they want to do is just to create something that is interesting. Right? . . . The result is that you have an attempt by people like Sarah, to not try to just subvert authority in the name of democracy, but to sort of have a more interesting voice than the voices that they hear around them. To do something new and different.

In fact, this is where MCA Denver may fall short, for their gallery presentations are not so new and different. Aside from the occasional mock-Russian avant-garde concept show, they take many pre-packaged traveling exhibitions and do not exert themselves unduly imagining how to improve their presentation. In the words of *Denver Post* Fine Arts critic Ray Mark Rinaldi: "The most interesting attractions aren't necessarily hanging on the walls." Lerner and Baie don't have much to say about that; ironically, even though connecting to audiences is essential to them, issues of gallery interpretation seem to elude their focus. Perhaps that feels too much like the overworked curator-educator dichotomy they left behind: a more onerous place to play—or not play at all.

Their strategy is to bypass the whole issue using a kind of halo effect. Speaking of their audience, Lerner says:

> They trust us enough, they don't feel alienated, they feel at home. So therefore, if they don't get some of this, fine. It's just like, you know, "Whatever: that's weird, but that's cool—I like *that*." And so that's what we really care about.

Such casual acceptance—a take it or leave it attitude—is not the voice of an outsider feeling excluded from some secret and elite knowledge. It's the voice of a viewer who feels comfortable, perhaps like an insider to contemporary art. To the extent the MCA can help its audience members feel like participants, they may circumvent the entire question of gallery interpretation, making an end run around the politics that have polarized so many museums.

> What kind of interpretation you put up . . . becomes irrelevant when you've created a feeling like: "You know what? This is a place that is, like, a lively place that's artful, that's spirited, that doesn't try to be elitist, that speaks to me, that I identify with."

If more established museums have their work cut out for them trying to connect traditional collections to contemporary life, the MCA uses the alternating current between high and low culture as the very rhythm of its heartbeat. Live programming—be it Mixed Taste talks, bison roasts, or performance—is one trend more and more museums are adopting to attract visitors. *Denver Post* critic Rinaldi has noticed:

> There is a striking coincidence between the "Art Fitness" training developed here and the "Art Fitness" educational program now offered by the Grand Rapids Museum of Art. Let's note that the MCA's trademark "Mixed Taste" series, which combines two unrelated topics into one weird lecture, closely resemble the dual-topic talks at the Museum of Fine Arts in Boston.
>
> And let's put on the record, cause it's a little strange, that the ridiculous and cheeky 2012 holiday video put out by the Art Institute of Chicago featuring its director Douglas Druick looks and sounds much like the ironic, holiday videos the MCA has been doing for three years with director Adam Lerner as the star. It's not as funny, though.[3]

The urgency of the moment and the contagion of human enthusiasm. If you're willing to do a collection bypass, these events can connect a culture-identified public with a conceptual playground every bit as engaging as the slides and tunnels of the City Museum, but designed with an older, more sophisticated, crowd in mind.

Key Takeaways

1. MCA Denver uses social practice as a tool to engage people in "the life of art." The live events are arguably more important and engaging than collections (it has none) or exhibitions.
2. The connection with audience takes place through a purposeful—and playful—dialogue between high and low culture. This is art as a jostling of ideas. An unsettling of orthodoxies.
3. In its gallery-based interpretation programs, the MCA does not innovate per se. Instead, they cultivate an attitude of fresh, irreverent play that deflates formality and empowers both staff and visitors to act creatively themselves.

Notes

1 The Lab. Past Programs. http://www.belmarlab.org/past-mixed.php Accessed October 7, 2014.
2 The Lab. History. http://belmarlab.org/history.php Accessed July 21, 2016.
3 Ray Mark Rinaldi. "Denver's Museum of Contemporary Art, a National Model for a Museum Possibilities." *The Denver Post*, February 1, 2013. http://www.denverpost.com/2013/01/31/denvers-museum-of-contemporary-art-a-national-model-for-a-museum-possibilities/ Accessed October 9, 2014.

Part Three

Conclusion

Varieties of Visitor-Centeredness
and Change

14 Conclusion

Varieties of Visitor-Centeredness and Organizational Change

There is not just one way to create a visitor-centered museum. Nor is there one best form of interpretive practice or one best type of museum change. Rather, the many ideas illustrated by these case studies suggest the breadth of creative possibilities available when taking on the challenge/opportunity of genuinely welcoming visitors into our galleries.

Our book title, *Creating the Visitor-Centered Museum*, incorporates both threads outlined at the outset: innovative visitor-centered practice and museum change. Fittingly, we now want to review these two themes and talk about lessons we have learned. Of course, easy prescriptions or magic bullets are hardly the purpose of this book. Instead, our goal is to share what we have witnessed and join or provoke the ongoing conversation related to how—or even why—museum professionals should prioritize visitors in our institutions.

Case Studies Continuum

We began our case studies with a continuum of approaches to practice we consider visitor-centered, regardless of whether the institutions themselves embrace that term.

At the heart of each approach is a philosophical stance, a set of convictions about how museums best fulfill their mission. With mission in mind,

Table 14.1 Continuum of Approaches to Connecting with Visitors

VISITOR-CENTERED MUSEUMS: A CONTINUUM OF APPROACHES

|............|_____|_____|_____|_____|_____|............|

| City Museum | Ruhr Museum | Minnesota History Ctr | Detroit Institute of Arts Kelvingrove Gallery | Denver Art Museum Columbus Art Museum Oakland Museum of CA | Van Abbe Museum | MCA Denver |

| PHYSICAL | IMMERSIVE | EMOTIVE | COGNITIVE + | CO-CREATIVE | META-COGNITIVE | |

museums make many choices, including the importance of audience focus and visitor research, what types of interpretive practices to use, and the kinds of staff roles and structural configurations to put into place. These decisions determine resource allocation and impact every aspect of a museum. The case studies highlight these varied elements and form the heart of this story.

With little focus on collection, City Museum showed us the value of play, participation, and creative exploration free of any explicitly articulated didactic framework. (Perhaps the closest they come is the sign at their admissions desk, which reads: *No maps.*) City's visionary founder Bob Cassilly perpetually reinvented the facility. His was a homegrown DIY ethos, generating an aesthetic more akin to Antoni Gaudí and Watts Tower than to standards of the contemporary art world.

Ruhr, another museum with a strong founder imprint, also focuses on experience, though there we find a different kind of immersive environment. The building design is put to stunning effect with a collection of objects showcased in unusual and moving ways. Through industrial reuse and design, Ruhr emphasizes the power of the local, but in this case as an opening onto a complex world of knowledge. Its message seems to be: Give me a geo-location—and a powerful structure—and I can speak forth the world.

As we move across the spectrum, we come to our final immersive, context-rich example, the Minnesota History Center. Here the theatrical and didactic are merged. Vivid simulations invite participation, and collection objects are included only when they serve to enhance the experience. Exhibitions are tested and refined to hook people (think Velcro) and teach them at the same time—with or without their being aware they are learning. In the world of science and history museums, these practices are common; not so with art museums.

These three immersive museums win us over by engaging us both physically and emotionally. Through design and masterful object dramaturgy, we connect with both local history and larger universal themes. We are moved— to imagine, remember, or learn. And sometimes just to play.

In the next group and in the bulk of museums we studied, we find traditional collection-based museums that have been reinvented for today's audiences. Each of these museums has evolved its own array of strategies for visitor engagement: at Denver, we find multiple forms of just-in-time didactics or video offerings; in Columbus, we see gallery-centric games and unusual juxtapositions of objects and ideas; in Oakland, we witness bold colors on the walls and clear, approachable texts in multiple languages; Glasgow Museums take their citywide service mandate to the next level with free entry, child-oriented viewing, and objects lent from their collection to local groups in portable, themed mini-exhibitions. Supporting visitor inclusion and even a sense of ownership, all of these traditional museums are committed to reimagining how their collections can best be presented to their diverse publics in ways that make them relevant to their lives.

At the Van Abbe, we find another collection-oriented museum, but one dedicated to provoking public awareness about the conventions of museum practice and each player's potential roles within it—even to the point of allowing contemporary artists to critique hallowed collection icons. The emphasis on meta-critique takes on a performative dimension at the MCA Denver, an institution untethered by collections. Here, a new generation leaves behind the polarized battles of its predecessors. It refuses to play the role of either curator or educator, and it reinvents museum practice at the intersection of high and low culture.

Interpretation and Provocations

Most of the visitor-oriented museums in our study integrate varied interpretive approaches as part of a new norm. Some of the most common components merit reprising:

1. When diverse groups of visitors come with varied needs and interests, multiple forms of interpretation are provided.
2. As "just in time" elements are the most effective, integration of interpretives into the galleries is essential.
3. While labels are not unproblematic, they are best when short and jargon-free (hiring outside writers is an interesting approach).
4. If dumbing down is a concern, we should design for different levels, novice and expert alike. Appreciate that all expertise is earned/learned.

We are also interested in the trend toward live programming. Expanding ways to connect with community, some institutions are reimagining the museum as a new kind of townsquare by offering programmed events, including festivals and concerts. The recent trend toward an expanded event-driven portfolio—whether live art performances in the galleries or late nights on a Thursday or Friday with food, drink, music, and activities—helps guarantee that visitors will have a good time at the museum. However, there is little guarantee that such visitor experiences will extend beyond the event and connect with the objects in the galleries unless we take steps to make our collections relevant as well.

Similarly, while technology-based interpretation can go a long way toward enriching certain visitors' experiences, it is only a piece of the puzzle. For some, it will never equal the appeal of live interpreters, be they docents, gallery hosts, or "game masters," who can act as powerful catalysts in changing museum-visitor relations.

Dan Spock, the Minnesota History Center's director, found that museum work is informed by a spirit of play—albeit sometimes, as in their World War II simulation, play that is serious as "Hell." Other museums also take quite literally naturalist Freeman Tilden's injunction that interpretation should act as a provocation—one "geared to the personality or experience of the visitor." Perhaps that is the very definition of "radical hospitality."

Museums' varied interpretive forms go a long way toward inviting visitors in—maybe even providing the provocation Tilden encourages. But just what kinds of provocation do visitors really want or need? Not surprisingly, this question does not yield easy answers.

The Curiosity–Driven Visitor

In her 1998 book *Paying Attention: Visitors and Museum Exhibitions*, Beverly Serrell described a class of museum-goers she dubbed "diligent visitors." These were people who viewed more than 51% of the elements, whether objects or didactics, in any given exhibition.[1] However, here is where the story gets more complicated. For example, even after Detroit's comprehensive reinstallation, studies suggest that gallery dwell times did not dramatically increase. We may ask: was the model itself faulty? More recent research indicates that only a small segment of audience, variously known by such psychographic profile names as Explorers, Fact Finders, or Hungry Minds, methodically moves through collection galleries, taking the objects in linear sequence and consuming the didactics provided. If this is the gold standard of behavior for which we are designing, might we be setting ourselves up for failure? By such standards, to quote museum researcher Jay Rounds, most "museum visitors . . . are not very good at visiting museums." In fact, as we have noted throughout, many visitors themselves share this belief.[2] Visitor malaise undoubtedly keeps many people away from our museums, but so too does our own lack of visitor understanding.

Rounds' research suggests that far more visitors follow a sort of random motion as they move through the galleries, careening from object to object. Building on Falk and Dierking's observation that "it is the expectation of novelty, the prediction that curiosity will be piqued and satisfied, that motivates most, if not all, free-choice learning," Rounds goes on to demonstrate that what appears at first glance to be erratic and unfocused behavior is in fact the most efficient way for casual visitors to take in a museum.[3]

He believes that, like animals foraging for food, museum visitors follow an "interest scent." Theirs is a constant trade-off between energy expended and success in finding objects that repay their attention.

> A curiosity-driven visitor who follows the sorts of rules described . . . is seen to be intelligent when our evaluation is based on the goals of the visitor, rather than those of the museum.

Rounds' statement about the curiosity-driven visitor offers us a shift in perspective: prioritizing visitors' agendas transforms them into active and intelligent agents. Furthermore, Rounds' work also suggests that by *not* focusing on visitors' interests, our work in the galleries might be missing the mark even when we develop elaborate interpretive resources.

Working from a Double Empathy

It is no longer sufficient to mount a scholarly and aesthetically impeccable collection presentation or exhibition that faithfully represents the artist or subject matter without acknowledging these essential questions: Did the majority of visitors understand what they were seeing? Did they "get" the show's thesis and key takeaways? Did they benefit from this experience? Did they feel more connected to the museum or, for that matter, the people they came with?

Factoring such questions into the calculus of exhibition success entails building in a culture of audience research and evaluation, with budgets and staff to support it. As we return again and again to the importance of audience research, we recognize that the best way to understand what works for visitors is simply to ask them.

In fact, for most of the museums we studied, a reliance on real-time feedback from audience research has become a regular part of exhibition development and design. Consider Minnesota and OMCA's reserving of gallery spaces expressly for prototyping ideas and testing them with target visitors, long before they even open an exhibition to the public. One of the most important lessons from this study is that audience research should be built into projects from the start.

In sum, we have come to appreciate that while the museum's agenda and expertise are still needed, they are by no means sufficient. To the extent we really want our collections and exhibitions to be meaningful to the audiences we have the privilege to serve, we must not only read and understand the objects in our care; we must read and comprehend our visitors as well.

Leading Organizational Change

The organizational changes taking place in these museums are as varied as are the forms of interpretation they practice. The new forms of teamwork that have evolved challenge everyone: directors, curators, educators, registrars, and designers alike. Significantly, most of these museums still find themselves renegotiating classical hierarchies.

Of Consultants and Props

Within many institutional cultures, habits and hierarchies are so entrenched that external consultants are necessary to offer an alternative view. Without such help, there is little room for movement, and change is much harder.

Former DIA in-house evaluator Matt Sikora mentions that consultants informed staff in many ways and aided in:

- teambuilding
- identifying "Big Ideas" for the galleries
- articulating visitor outcomes

- label-writing
- designing for conversation
- facilitating visitor panels and the debriefing sessions that followed
- devising evaluation methods

Detroit was unusual in having two in-house evaluators on staff at the time of its reinstallation. They also served in a consulting capacity to the interdepartmental teams as they tried out Big Ideas and exhibition interpretives. At other museums such as Denver and OMCA, curators and educators work with both external and internal evaluators, distinguishing between "Big-E" and "small-e" evaluation, the former being grant-funded studies and the latter consisting of just-in-time gallery interventions in which staff lead structured conversations with a small visitor sample to get rapid feedback on activity mockups or label language. As audience research becomes ever more important, this area of consultant input—and in-house capacity building—also continues to grow.

Recognizing some of the difficulties associated with organizational change, OMCA hired an outside consultant who shared information and theories about organizational change with the staff so all could gain perspective on the process. Lori Fogarty says:

> And so she presented a chart [adapted from Figure 3.1 on page 33] that is like the Stages of Change . . . kind of encouraging people to think about where they are on this, and knowing, one, that it's just a natural thing, that even though people may be frustrated that we don't have all the answers, how could we? We're still in this change process.

The chart was helpful in aiding staff to understand that change takes time and that one can feel excited about the future and at the same time scared of losing the past. The OMCA team also developed a document specifically designed to help guide them.

> We're calling it the Owner's Manual . . . it's about this transformation process of reorganizing . . . [We] did a lot of reading about change processes, as part of this. And we are aware—you know, a lot of this literature calls it the neutral zone, which is you've given up the old, but you're not quite there at the new yet. And it's a hard time, because processes aren't in place and systems that you think should be easy aren't, and people are still trying to figure out where they are and what their job is.

Learning about a "neutral zone" makes it easier for museum staff to deal with the uncertainties inherent in change. In addition to offering perspective and expertise, consultants play an invaluable role by reassuring staff about common growing pains.

While outside consultants are often important, ultimately it comes back to leadership. Where we found innovative ideas being implemented, we also found strong leadership. In fact, the importance of leadership in creating a visitor-centered museum can hardly be overstated and it warrants special attention.

Growing into Leadership, Staying the Course

Most leaders did not start out seeking change or seeing themselves at the forefront of institutional transformation. A director talks about her experience:

> I wouldn't have thought, necessarily, that I would be at the forefront of the risk taking . . . and being the one to, not make always the most popular decisions, at least in the moment, or really be at the bow on the ship, going through and saying, "Okay, we're going to do this and it's going to be hard, or it's a risk, or we don't know how this is going to turn out."

While a long successful career had prepared this director for the rigors ahead, earlier she had been more deferential to curators:

> I would say I was pretty deferential to the curators. I felt like it was my job to make things that they wanted to do happen. And I didn't really question what those things were. I didn't question much about the mission. Now I feel like I have to have a balance. I certainly still see my role as being supportive and facilitating and coaching the curatorial staff and the staff at large. But I also think I'm now in more of a role myself of being the provocateur and saying, "This isn't where this institution is going and you really need to think about this in a different way; or you need to balance, you know, what you're trying to do with this perspective."

Museum directors who mandate change come up against stiff resistance from both within and, in some cases, without. As directors take on new leadership roles, the need to reinforce a visitor-centered mandate becomes increasingly clear, and they persevere, inspiring staff and board to reform their priorities.[4] For example, recognizing the challenge inherent in creating new cross-disciplinary teams, one director talks about a consultant's warning to him after a staff retreat:

> He [the consultant] said, "Why are you doing this? You've got wonderful art on the walls, you've got great stuff, and this is going to be very hard." And my answer is that if the whole staff isn't buying into this, it's not going to work. It's still not the case, but that's the goal, to have everyone understanding that they are part of this whole—that they are part of the whole effort, and that an unpleasant experience in a bathroom because the janitor didn't clean it properly is going to have as much effect, and maybe even more, than swooning in front of a work

of art. So you know, it had to be a complete institutional thing. So the evaluators are in the middle. It's not just the art that they're evaluating; it's the whole visitor experience. And that includes the staff experience.

This director is clear about the importance of his holistic vision. The consultant's question—"Why are you doing this?"—did not scare him off from his chosen path. Secure in the belief that change is necessary, such leaders are willing to take risks on behalf of their vision, their public, and their institutional mission.

Creating a Thriving Learning Culture

Leaders who take risks themselves make risk-taking part of the museum culture. Not incidentally, such bold initiatives help create a museum culture that welcomes experimentation and collaboration, providing ground ripe for innovation. With their focus on creating an environment where visitors thrive, bold directors spur the kind of culture where staff can thrive as well.

A curator at the Van Abbe Museum praises her director for creating a culture that embraces mistakes and risk taking.

> Our director is a person who really put this in the museum, like we should experiment, we should be radical. It's allowed . . . It's allowed, to make mistakes. Please, make your U-turns. If you make a mistake, just tell it. Or that you missed something or you did some—Tell it. Don't try to hide it or soft [pedal] it. Maybe it's even good for something, that we can all learn something from it and we should do it differently.

While many institutions see themselves as valuing innovation, creative ideas need space and support to develop; they need a cultural norm that values experimentation. As one curator points out, this new kind of experimental culture is not about praising the individual—or as she puts it, "star protecting." Rather, it's about valuing how staff members' varied skills all contribute to producing high quality work. Mutual respect lies at the core of any team's success. Openness and collaboration, not just trial and error, foster innovation. That said, open dialogue also needs leadership. In the words of Dan Spock:

> The key to leading teamwork is to create an environment where very different people can bring their best game, where it's safe to disagree, where differences are engaged openly and forthrightly, and where these differences can be worked through and synthesized to an optimal result. . . . Teams can easily fall into dysfunction on one end and groupthink at the other end, so the art of it hinges on processes where differences are not stuffed down, but are heard and processed thoughtfully and openly.

Whether intervening to keep dialogue fruitful, keeping new label-writing processes on track, or ensuring that the team doesn't get bogged down by internal fighting, all the leaders we encountered recognized the importance of supporting team dialogue. Leaders are tactful, even artful, in how they do this. These directors also understand the need to make hard choices. Spock again:

> I do think our best work has been the product of the best collective thinking along with some ruthless decisiveness at critical times.

Sometimes, when all else fails, the hard choice is to let go of staff who refuse to align with the museum's new direction.

Living with Ambiguity

The approaches adopted by these museums cover a broad spectrum. As previously noted, many of the changes described here began to occur in certain museums as far back as the late 1980s. Museum consultant and evaluator Randi Korn traces the roots:

> In the late 1980s, exhibition development in many museums changed from being a curatorial project to an interdisciplinary team project . . . For the first time, educators and evaluators, among others, were invited to work with content specialists during exhibition development.

This was the "Kellogg Model," where a curator, an educator, and a designer worked together, instead of a linear handoff from curator to designer to educator. For many, that model has become synonymous with teamwork in museums. However, even the most die-hard advocates for changing the ways museums do business say that simply adopting a team approach does not guarantee more successful exhibitions.

Kathleen McLean notes that the team approach was "neither the magic bullet nor a guarantee for excellent exhibitions," while Korn says, "No one has conducted a study to determine whether the team approach creates exhibitions that are more visitor-centered than the curator-centered approach."[5] "If there's one person who doesn't buy into the process, development gets thrown off and we're not doing our best work," says the DIA's manager of interpretation, Swarupa Anila.

Finding the right tools to reach audiences takes time while testing reveals what works and what can still be improved. OMCA director Lori Fogarty comments:

> And I think the other thing that for us is very important is to know that I don't know if any of these are the right tools . . . I think what we have to be willing to do is try some of those tools, then ask the right questions of our public.

Although we might wish for a simple set of received recipes or best practices, we might have to rely on processes without predetermined outcomes. In the words of MNHS's Dan Spock:

> I don't like the idea of everything gravitating toward a predictable, or best-practices model. I think best practices is kind of a chimera. You know, it's sort of a phantom idea, and it could spell mediocrity. And so I think, you know, there's the best practice for the project; but not necessarily this idea of developing, you know, accreditation, broad breast.

Korn adds this warning, indicative of the risks inherent in any paradigm shift: "People who participate in exhibition teams find the process messy and frustrating, but also invigorating and stimulating." Curators are not alone in having to accept the uncertainty that comes with change. In truth, there really are no easy answers when creating a museum that works for all. These issues remain challenging and complex.

Moving Forward

How can we encourage more museums to offer experiences that are rich and emotionally complex for a broad public? What will it take to make that change?

Training Up

Better training is part of the answer. While educators are routinely trained to consider audience, curators are not. Columbus's Nannette Maciejunes, who was a curator herself for many decades,[6] explains:

> I think we've got a mismatch between training and expectation. I think we've got to integrate the education vision and the curatorial vision and the visitor experience more effectively.

OMCA curator René de Guzman confirms the current disconnect:

> I'm an adjunct professor for a curatorial studies program. I've taught a number of semesters, and every time I ask the students: Has anyone ever mentioned the word *visitor* to you? Not a word. . . . You have to train curators up.

What, we might ask, is the training they're currently getting? A recent catalogue of courses at the Bard Center for Curatorial Studies, which specifically serves the art world, reveals:

> subjects of inquiry including, but not limited to: globalization; modes of networks and distribution; technology and aesthetics; spatial

politics; new institutionalism; social practice; and artistic and archival research.

None of the required courses in the two-year masters program encompass either Visitor Studies or Oral and Written—much less Media—Communication for a lay audience; among the nine electives mentioned, only one, "the sociology of museums and their audiences," even alludes to visitors.[7]

Similarly, in doctoral programs that train the history, science, or art museum curators of the future, one does not find the courses that constitute the core curriculum of Museum Studies:

- History and Theory of Museums
- The Visitor Experience: Learning Theories and Understanding Audiences
- The Visitor Experience: Interpretive Methods and Applications
- Museums and Communities
- Museums, Interactive Technology and Electronic Access[8]

A more effective training might also add to these the increasingly important subjects of design thinking and managing organizational change, both of which are at the heart of responsive teamwork in the twenty-first century.

In the words of one curator critical of museum intransigence:

> A lot of this is kind of this weird sociology. You know, it's like museums move forward not because there's any sort of real law or AAM's going to discredit you if you put a comfortable bench in the gallery. It's just custom . . . this weird museum society custom.

The adherence to customs that endure simply out of habit sells museums short on their ability to adapt with the times and create vital, new, team-based approaches that make use of the various forms of expertise they already have on staff and the new ones they need to cultivate.

With a younger generation ready to move things forward, attention to how we educate them becomes a priority.

Taking the Long View

Our study suggests there is a side benefit to expanding our reach and listening to the needs of infrequent and non-visitors. As we succeed in welcoming new audiences, internal organizational change is not the only form of change we see. Rather, the culture of our museums themselves will inevitably change. In other words, the change we see happening may be even more far-reaching and robust than first appears.

We believe that while creating a "visitor-centered" museum is not easy or straightforward, it is nonetheless worthwhile. The more we understand our shifting constituencies, the better equipped we will be to grow along with them. With the long view in mind, caring about the visitors' agendas only better prepares us to evolve over time and remain a valued and meaningful cultural resource.

Creating a visitor-centered museum is a hard choice that grows out of a sense of duty to the public. Ultimately, it is a decision to accept the responsibility that comes with being keepers of the public culture.

This book is about facing the real challenges of visitor-centered museums and promoting a conversation about them. *What if* you find only 5–12% of your visitors read your wall texts? *What if* the critics say you are dumbing down? *What if* staff don't get along? What do you do then? Rather than offer simple answers, we urge colleagues to ask the questions and discuss them openly and vulnerably, the better to move forward together.

In this book we seek to effect change. By sharing these stories we hope to inspire colleagues who, like us, value the contributions visitors have to offer. We believe that creating a visitor-centered museum is not only worthwhile, but essential to the sustainability of our field. We hope the task is better undertaken with the help of these experienced and committed colleagues, who can help chart the rough waters. We hope these exemplars serve as a guide and companion as well as an important prompt to the emergent dialogue that is finally required.

Notes

1 In fact, the 2003 tracking and timing observations conducted in the galleries of the Detroit Institute of Arts fell so far short of this standard that they helped build institutional consensus around the need for the interpretive overhaul we see in the DIA's galleries today.
2 Marilyn Hood. "Staying Away: Why People Choose Not to Visit Museums." *Museum News* 61, 4 (April 1983): 50–57.
3 Jay Rounds. "Strategies for the Curiosity-Driven Museum Visitor." *Curator: The Museum Journal* 47, 4 (October 2004): 389–412.
4 In many cases, they don't have a choice. Many of the museums we studied were off the beaten track (e.g., Detroit, Denver, Columbus, and Oakland). This proves to be a mixed blessing. On the one hand, it gives them a freedom their counterparts in major art world centers do not have; on the other, it also makes the obligation to meet their publics "where they are" quite real—and crucial to their survival.
5 Randi Korn. "The Case for Holistic Intentionality." *Curator: The Museum Journal* 50, 2 (April 2007): 225–264.
6 Maciejunes worked for decades as a curator before becoming a director responsible for the well-being of her entire institution.
7 Bard Center for Curatorial Studies: Master of Arts Program in Curatorial Studies. Catalog. Annandale-on-Hudson: Bard College, 2013, p. 8.
8 Excerpted from course listing for Master of Arts in Museum Studies, John F. Kennedy University. http://www.jfku.edu/Programs-and-Courses/College-of-Graduate-Professional-Studies/Museum-Studies/Programs/MA-Museum-Studies.html Accessed October 15, 2014.

Appendix A
Method

More than fifty colleagues from North America and Europe were asked to nominate museums with exemplary interpretive practices regardless of size or type. In selecting our final set to visit we emphasized art museums (as they are a special interest), but kept in mind that other kinds of museums have been pioneering visitor-centered approaches for years, approaches from which all museum practitioners might have much to learn.

In-Depth: Site Visit + Interviews	*Site Visit Only***
Oakland Museum of California	Tropenmuseum, Amsterdam
Detroit Institute of Arts	Amstelkring, Amsterdam
Columbus Museum of Art	Boijmans van Beuningen, Rotterdam
Ruhr Museum, Essen, Germany	Museum Insel Hombroich, Neuss, Germany
Van Abbe Museum, Eindhoven, NL	Riverside Museum, Glasgow
Kelvingrove Gallery, Glasgow, UK	Gallery of Modern Art, Glasgow
Denver Art Museum	Nitshill Open Storage Facility, Glasgow
Museum of Contrary Art, Denver*	Walker Art Center, Minneapolis
Minnesota History Center	Minneapolis Institute of Arts
City Museum, St. Louis	The Pulitzer Foundation, St. Louis

 * Site not studied in depth; select interviews conducted only.
 ** We availed ourselves of the opportunity to visit other museums in the locales of our targeted sites, without conducting interviews with their staff or including them in the study.

Interview Subjects	*Number*
Museum Directors	11
Curators	7
Educators-Interpretive Specialists	7
Cross-Departmental Teams	7

Subjects Interviewed, total n=32

Interviews

Drawing on social science techniques, we sought nominations from the field and developed a roster of museums to visit and individuals to interview. We were not seeking a random collection, but a purposeful list (Patton, 1990). The target population is the larger group of innovative visitor-centered museums, although part of the purpose of this work is to better understand the bounds of this group.

We crafted an interview protocol gleaned from social science techniques (Miles and Huberman, 1994; Gardner, Gregory, Csikszentmihalyi, Damon and Michaelson, 1997, 2001) and refined from testing in the field. We used a one-hour semi-structured interview as the primary data source, while additional measures such as personal notes and papers supplemented the transcripts. To situate the work, we rely on visitor research and literature about change in museums.

Making Sense of the Data

As suggested by Maxwell and others (Maxwell, 1992; Miles and Huberman, 1994), on completion of each interview we wrote reflective memos describing the setting and initial thoughts about the interview.

In lieu of formal coding, we used two focused readings and a series of discussions to generate themes. First reading: We read and annotated each interview and added observations to our initial reflections. Second reading: We reviewed each transcript and together considered additional themes that surfaced. As our goal has always been to be descriptive, rather than comprehensive, we make no generalizing claims. Also, keeping our audience in mind, we chose to blend approaches, settling on something more journalistic than scientific.

Appendix B
Adult Gallery Activities at the Denver Art Museum

Getting Adults to Notice

1. The object to be used has to draw attention to itself, not just "sit quietly on a table."
2. It must be clear what the activity is about—immediately.
3. The activity must be designed to look "adult."

Criteria for Successful Activities (Satisfy Some or All)

1. Produce a memento of the museum visit.
2. Foster a personally meaningful connection with the art.
3. Make it easy to be successful.
4. Have an adult look.
5. Keep it open-ended.
6. Design it to be somewhat intuitive.
7. Make it low maintenance and self-directed.
8. Use conservation-safe supplies.[1]
9. Build in staff time to go through twice a day, check things, restock them, and make sure they work.[2]

Notes

1 These tips are adapted from Daryl Fischer and Lisa Levinson. "Redefining Successful Interpretation in Art Museums." *Curator: The Museum Journal* 53, 3 (July 2010): 307–308.
2 Melora McDermott-Lewis bluntly reinforces Fischer and Levinson's point: "If you put it out there, it can't look crummy."

Appendix C
Make-Up of DIA Visitor Panels

Location

Locals   (tri-county area)   100%

Level of Expertise

Novices   60%
Advanced Amateurs   30%
Experts   10%

Relationship to DIA (Averaged Over 3 Panels)

DIA visitors   60–70%
Non-visitors   30–40%
FAMILIES (elem-high) school   50%

Age

Seniors   30%
Under 30   20%
30–60   50%

Bibliography

Adams, Marianna and Beverly Serrell. *Phase 2 Summative Evaluation of DIA Interpretive Strategies*. Detroit: Detroit Institute of Arts, 2012.

Association of Art Museum Curators: Mission and History. http://www.artcurators.org/?History

Bard Center for Curatorial Studies. *Master of Arts Program in Curatorial Studies*. Catalog. Annandale-on-Hudson: Bard College, 2013.

Baxter, Liam. Untitled post to GlasgowGuide online forum dated March 2, 2011. http://discuss.glasgowguide.co.uk/lofiversion/index.php/t20239.html

Becker, Howard S. *Art Worlds*. Berkeley: University of California Press, 1982.

Bedford, Leslie. *The Art of Museum Exhibitions*. Walnut Creek: Left Coast Press, Inc., 2014.

Bitgood, Stephen. *Social Design in Museums: The Psychology of Visitor Studies*, Volume 1. Edinburgh and Cambridge: MuseumsEtc, 2011.

Blackmon, Carolyn P., Teresa K. LaMaster, Lisa C. Roberts, and Beverly Serrell. *Open Conversations: Strategies for Professional Development in Museums*. Chicago: Field Museum of Natural History, 1988.

Blythe, Sarah Ganz and Barbara Palley. "'Reading the Walls': A Study of Curatorial Expectation and Visitor Perception." In *Museum Gallery Interpretation and Material Culture*, edited by Juliette Fritsch. London and New York: Routledge, 2011, pp. 221–233.

Borgelt, Christiane and Regina Jost. *Zollverein World Heritage Site Essen*. Berlin: Stadtwandel Verlag, 2009.

Bourdieu, Pierre. *Distinction: A Social Critique of the Judgment of Taste*. Translated by Richard Nice. Cambridge MA: Harvard University Press, 1984.

Chambers, Marlene. "Is Anyone Out There? Audience and Communication." *Museum News* 62 (June 1984): 47–54.

Chambers, Marlene. "Sometimes More Is Too Much." In "Focus on the Detroit Institute of Arts," Peter Linett (Ed.), *Curator: The Museum Journal* 52, 1 (January 2006): 67–76.

Csikszentmihalyi, Mihalyi. "Notes on Art Museum Experiences." In Getty Center for Education in the Arts and J. Paul Getty Museum, *Insights: Museums, Visitors, Attitudes, Expectations: A Focus Group Experiment*. Malibu, CA: J. Paul Getty Trust, 1991, pp. 123–131.

Davis, Jessica, Brenda Leach, and Mimi Michaelson. *The MUSE Book: A Report on the Work of Project MUSE*. Harvard Graduate School of Education. Project Zero. Project MUSE, 1996.

Dawber, Stephen. "Blairism on the Walls at Kelvingrove." *Variant* 27. http://www.variant.org.uk/27texts/kelvingrove27.html

DeSantis, Karin and Abigail Housen. "A Brief Guide to Developmental Theory and Aesthetic Development." New York: Visual Understanding in Education, 2009. http://vtshome.org/research/articles-other-readings

Dissanayake, Ellen. *Homo Aestheticus*. Seattle: University of Washington Press, 1995.

Duke, Linda. "The Museum Visit: It's an Experience, Not a Lesson." *Curator* 53, 3 (July 2010): 271–279.

Durbin, Gail. "The Educational Basis for the Galleries." In *Creating the British Galleries at the V&A: A Study in Museology*, edited by Christopher Wilk and Nick Humphrey. London: V&A Publications and Goppion, 2004, pp. 37–47.

Economou, Maria. *Evaluation Strategy for the Re-Development of the Displays and Visitor Facilities at the Museum and Art Gallery, Kelvingrove*. Glasgow: University of Glasgow Humanities Advanced Technology and Information Institute, 1999.

Esche, Charles. "Start with a Table . . ." In Paul O'Neill and Mick Wilson (Eds.), *Curating and the Educational Turn*. London and Amsterdam: Open Editions and de Appel, 2010, pp. 310–319.

Esche, Charles and De Appel CP. "Stand I Don't." In *Curating and the Educational Turn*, edited by Paul O'Neill and Mick Wilson. London and Amsterdam: Open Editions and de Appel, 2010, pp. 297–309.

Falk, John H. *Identity and the Museum Visitor Experience*. Walnut Creek, CA: Left Coast Press, Inc., 2009.

Falk, John H. "The Museum Experience: Who Visits, Why and to What Effect?" In *Reinventing the Museum: The Evolving Conversation on the Paradigm Shift*, edited by Gail Anderson. Lanham: AltaMira Press; 2nd Edition, 2012, pp. 317–329.

Falk, John H. and Lynn D. Dierking. *The Museum Experience Revisited*. Walnut Creek, CA: Left Coast Press, Inc., 2013.

Faria, Mary T. "Inviting Visitors into the Conversation about Art: Labels." In *How We Visitors Changed Our Museum: Transforming the Gallery of California Art at the Oakland Museum of California*, edited by Barbara Henry and Kathleen McLean. Oakland: OMCA, 2010, pp. 31–44.

Fischer, Daryl. "Denver Art Museum IMLS Project Front-End Visitor Panel Debriefing Meeting Report." Grand Haven: Musynergy, 2012, p. 3.

Fischer, Daryl and Lisa Levinson. "Redefining Successful Interpretation in Art Museums." *Curator: The Museum Journal* 53, 3 (July 2010): 307–308.

Fraser, Andrea and Alexander Alberro (Eds.). *Museum Highlights: The Writings of Andrea Fraser*. Cambridge: MIT Press, 2007.

Fritsch, Juliette. "'Education Is a Department Isn't It?' Perceptions of Education, Learning and Interpretation in Exhibition Development." In *Museum Gallery Interpretation and Material Culture*, edited by Juliette Fritsch. London and New York: Routledge, 2011, pp. 234–248.

Gardner, Howard. *Frames of Mind: The Theory of Multiple Intelligences*. New York: Basic Books, 1983.

Gardner, Howard, Anne Gregory, Mihaly Csikszentmihalyi, William Damon, and Mimi Michaelson. "The Empirical Basis of Good Work: Methodological Considerations." In *Good Work Project Report Series*, edited by Jeff Solomon. Number 3, Project Zero. Cambridge, MA: Harvard University, 1997 (2001).

Getty Center for Education in the Arts and the J. Paul Getty Museum. *Insights: Museums, Visitors, Attitudes, Expectations.* Los Angeles: The J. Paul Getty Trust, 1991.

Gurian, Elaine Heumann. *Civilizing the Museum: The Collected Writings of Elaine Heumann Gurian.* London and New York: Routledge, 2006.

Gurian, Elaine Heumann. "Exhibitions: Kelvingrove Art Gallery and Museum, Glasgow, Scotland." *Curator: The Museum Journal*, 50, 3 (July 2007): 358–361.

Halpin, Marjorie M. "'Play It again, Sam': Reflections on a New Museology." In *Museums and Their Communities*, edited by Sheila Watson. London and New York: Routledge, 2007, pp. 47–52.

Ham, Sam H. "Meaning Making—The Premise and Promise of Interpretation." Keynote address to Scotland's First National Conference on Interpretation, Royal Botanic Gardens, Edinburgh, April 4, 2002. http://www.researchgate.net/publication/242763042_Meaning_Making—The_Premise_and_Promise_of_Interpretation

Heath, Chip and Dan Heath. *Made to Stick: Why Some Ideas Survive and Others Die.* New York: Random House, 2007.

Hein, George. *Learning in the Museum.* London and New York: Routledge, 1998.

Helguera, Pablo. *Education for Socially Engaged Art: A Materials and Techniques Handbook.* New York: Jorge Pinto Books, 2011.

Henry, Barbara and Kathleen McLean (Eds.). *How We Visitors Changed Our Museum: Transforming the Gallery of California Art at the Oakland Museum of California.* Oakland: Oakland Museum of California, 2010.

Hood, Marilyn G. "Staying Away: Why People Choose Not to Visit Museums." *Museum News* 61, 4 (April 1983): 50–57.

Housen, Abigail. "Art Viewing and Aesthetic Development: Designing for the Viewer." In *From Periphery to Center: Art Museum Education in the 21st Century*, edited by Pat Villenueve. Reston: National Art Education Association, 2007. http://vtshome.org/research/articles-other-readings

Kirshenblatt-Gimblett, Barbara. "Exhibitionary Complexes." In Ivan Karp, Corinne A. Kratz, Lynn Szwaja, and Tómas Ybarra-Frausto (Eds.), *Museum Frictions: Public Cultures/Global Transformations.* Durham and London: Duke, 2006, pp. 35–45.

Knutson, Karen. "Creating a Space for Learning: Curators, Educators, and the Implied Audience." In *Learning Conversations in Museums*, edited by Gaea Leinhardt, Kevin Crowley, and Karen Knutson. Mahwah, NJ: Lawrence Erlbaum Associates, Inc., 2002.

Korn, Randi. "The Case for Holistic Intentionality." *Curator: The Museum Journal* 50, 2 (April 2007): 225–264.

Kotter, John P. "Leading Change: Why Transformation Efforts Fail." In *Reinventing the Museum: The Evolving Conversation on the Paradigm Shift*, edited by Gail Anderson. Lanham: AltaMira Press; 2nd Edition, 2012, pp. 521–531.

Latimer, Sue. "Art for Whose Sake?" In *Museum Gallery Interpretation and Material Culture*, edited by Juliette Fritsch. London: Routledge, 2011, pp. 67–77.

Liedtka, Jeanne M. and Randy Salzman. "Leading Innovation at Kelvingrove." University of Virginia Darden School Foundation, 2009. Darden Case No. UVA-S-0162. Available at http://ssrn.com/abstract=1584555

Linett, Peter. "Reinstallation Rorshach: What Do You See in the Renovated Detroit Institute of Arts?" Editor's preface to special issue: "Focus on the Detroit Institute of Arts." *Curator: The Museum Journal* 52, 1 (January 2009): 5–12.

Loos, Ted. "Hi, Let's Talk Art. No, Really, It's My Job." *The New York Times*, August 6, 2006. http://www.nytimes.com/2006/08/06/college/coll06loos.html. Accessed March 1, 2015.

MacGregor, Gordon. "Benighted at the Museum." *Scottish Review*: http://www.scottishreview.net/GMacGregor212.html

Mannion, Shelley, Amalia Sabiescu, and William Robinson, "An Audio State of Mind: Understanding Behaviour Around Audio Guides and Visitor Media." *MW2015: Museums and the Web 2015*. February 1, 2015. http://mw2015.museums andtheweb.com/paper/an-audio-state-of-mind-understanding-behviour-around-audio-guides-and-visitor-media/ Accessed August 16, 2015.

Marincola, Paula (Ed.). *What Makes a Great Exhibition?* Philadelphia: Philadelphia Exhibitions Initiative, 2006.

Maxwell, J. A. *Qualitative Research Design: An Interactive Approach: Applied Social Research Methods Series*, Volume 41. Thousand Oaks, CA: Sage Publications, 1996.

McDermott-Lewis, Melora. *The Denver Art Museum Interpretive Project*. Denver: Denver Art Museum, 1990.

McKenna-Cress, Polly and Janet A. Kamien. *Creating Exhibitions: Collaboration in the Planning, Development, and Design of Innovative Experiences*. Hoboken, NJ: John Wiley & Sons, 2013.

McLean, Kathleen and Wendy Pollock. *The Convivial Museum*. Washington, DC: Association of Science-Technology Centers Incorporated, 2010.

McLeod, Fiona (Ed.). *Essential Kelvingrove*. London: Glasgow Museums Publishing in association with Philip Wilson Publishers, 2010.

Miles, M. B. and A. M. Huberman. *Qualitative Data Analysis: An Expanded Source Book*. Thousand Oaks, CA: Sage Publications; 2nd Edition, 1994.

Nakamura, Jeanne. "The Nature of Vital Engagement in Adulthood." In *Supportive Frameworks for Youth Engagement*, edited by Mimi Michaelson and Jeanne Nakamura. San Francisco: Jossey-Bass, 2001, pp. 5–18.

Nelson, Karen. "Seeing Ourselves in the Gallery of California Art." In *How We Visitors Changed Our Museum: Transforming the Gallery of California Art at the Oakland Museum of California*, edited by Barbara Henry and Kathleen McLean. Oakland: Oakland Museum of California, 2010, pp. 61–65.

Newman, Alan. "Report: What Did the Focus Groups Reveal?" In Getty Center for Education in the Arts and J. Paul Getty Museum, *Insights: Museums, Visitors, Attitudes, Expectations: A Focus Group Experiment*. Malibu, CA: J. Paul Getty Trust, 1991, pp. 112–122.

Obrist, Hans Ulrich. *A Brief History of Curating*. Zurich: JRP | Ringier and Dijon: Les Presses du reel, 2008.

O'Doherty, Brian. *Inside the White Cube: The Ideology of the Gallery Space*. San Francisco: Lapis Press, 1986.

O'Neill, Mark. "Cultural Attendance and Public Mental Health: From Research to Practice." *Journal of Public Mental Health* 9, 4 (2010): 22–29.

O'Neill, Mark. "Kelvingrove: Telling Stories in a Treasured Old/New Museum." *Curator: The Museum Journal* 50, 4 (October 2007): 379–397.

O'Neill, Mark. "Preface." In the Research Centre for Museums and Galleries in the Department of Museum Studies at the University of Leicester, *A Catalyst for Change: The Social Impact of the Open Museum*. Leicester: Research Centre for Museums and Galleries, University of Leicester, 2002, p. 2.

Patterson, Kerry, Joseph Grenny, Ron McMillan, and Al Switzler. *Crucial Conversations: Tools for Talking When Stakes Are High*. New York: McGraw Hill, 2012.

Patton, Michael Quinn. *Qualitative Evaluation & Research Methods*. Newbury Park, CA: Sage Publications; 2nd edition, 1990.

Pekarik, Andrew J., Z. D. Doering, and D. A. Karns. "Exploring Satisfying Experiences in Museums." *Curator: The Museum Journal* 42, 2 (April 1999): 152–173.

Pekarik, Andrew J. and Barbara Mogel. "Ideas, Objects, or People? A Smithsonian Exhibition Team Views Visitors Anew." *Curator: The Museum Journal* 53, 4 (October 2010): 465–482.

Penney, David. "Reinventing the Detroit Institute of Arts: The Reinstallation Project 2002–2007." In "Focus on the Detroit Institute of Arts," ed. Peter Linett, special issue, *Curator: The Museum Journal* 52, 1 (January 2006): 35–44.

Phillips, Will. "Institution-Wide Change in Museums." In *Transforming Practice: Selections from the Journal of Museum Education, 1992–1999*, edited by Joanne S. Hirsch and Lois H. Silverman. Washington, DC: Museum Education Roundtable, 2000, pp. 71–78.

Pitman, Bonnie and Ellen Hirzy. *Ignite the Power of Art*. New Haven and London: Yale University Press and Dallas Museum of Art, 2010.

Rand, Judy. "The 227-Mile Museum, or, Why We Need a Visitors' Bill of Rights." *Visitor Studies Association*, 1996. http://w.informalscience.org/images/research/VSA-a0a0x9-a_5730.pdf. Reprinted in *Curator: The Museum Journal* 44, 1 (January 2001): 7–14.

Ray, Mark Rinaldi. "Denver's Museum of Contemporary Art, a National Model for a Museum Possibilities." *The Denver Post*, February 1, 2013. http://www.denverpost.com/2013/01/31/denvers-museum-of-contemporary-art-a-national-model-for-a-museum-possibilities/

Rice, Danielle. "Balancing Act: Education and the Competing Impulses of Museum Work." In "Museum Education at the Art Institute of Chicago," special issue, *Art Institute of Chicago Museum Work* 29, 1: 6–19, 90.

Roberts, Lisa. *From Knowledge to Narrative: Education and the Changing Museum*. Washington: Smithsonian Books, 1997.

Roberts, Lisa C. "Educators on Exhibit Teams: A New Role, a New Era." In *Transforming Practice: Selections from the Journal of Museum Education, 1992–1999*, edited by Joanne S. Hirsch and Lois H. Silverman. Washington, DC: Museum Education Roundtable, 2000, pp. 89–97.

Roberts, Lisa C. "Changing Practices of Interpretation." In *Reinventing the Museum: The Evolving Conversation on the Paradigm Shift*, edited by Gail Anderson. Lanham: AltaMira Press; 2nd Edition, 2012, pp. 144–162.

Roppola, Tiina. *Designing for the Museum Visitor Experience*. London and New York: Routledge, 2012.

Rounds, Jay. "Strategies for the Curiosity-Driven Museum Visitor." *Curator: The Museum Journal* 47, 4 (October 2004): 389–412.

Salgado, Mariana. *Designing for an Open Museum*. Jyväskylä, Finland: University of Art and Design Helsinki, 2009.

Samis, P. "Gaining Traction in the Vaseline: Visitor Response to a Multi-Track Interpretation Design for *Matthew Barney: DRAWING RESTRAINT*." In *Museums and the Web 2007: Proceedings*, edited by J. Trant and D. Bearman. Toronto: Archives & Museum Informatics, published March 1, 2007 http://www.archimuse.com/mw2007/papers/samis/samis.html

Samis, Peter. "New Technologies as Part of a Comprehensive Interpretive Plan." In *The Digital Museum: A Think Guide*, edited by Phyllis Hecht and Herminia Din. Washington, DC: American Association of Museums, 2007, pp. 19–34. Also published as "Visual Velcro: Hooking the Visitor." *Museum News* 86, no. 6 (Nov–Dec 2007): 57–62, 68–71.

Samis, Peter. "The Exploded Museum." In *Digital Technologies and the Museum Experience*, edited by Loïc Tallon and Kevin Walker. Walnut Creek, CA: Alta Mira, 2008, pp. 3–18.

Samis, Peter and Stephanie Pau. "After the Heroism, Collaboration: Organizational Learning and the Mobile Space." In *Museums and the Web 2009: Proceedings*, edited by Jennifer Trant and David Bearman. Toronto: Archives & Museum Informatics, 2009. http://www.archimuse.com/mw2009/papers/samis/samis.html

Samis, Peter and Mimi Michaelson. "Meaning-Making in Nine Acts." In *Exhibitionist* 32, 1 (Spring 2013): 54–59.

Serrell, Beverly. *Exhibit Labels: An Interpretive Approach*. Walnut Creek, CA: AltaMira Press, 1996.

Serrell, Beverly. *Judging Exhibitions: A Framework for Assessing Excellence*. Walnut Creek: Left Coast Press, Inc., 2006.

Sharmacharja, Shamita (Ed). *A Manual for the 21st Century Art Institution*. London: Koenig Books, 2009.

Sheikh, Simon. "Letter to Jane (Investigation of a Function)." In *Curating and the Educational Turn*, edited by Paul O'Neill and Mick Wilson. London and Amsterdam: Open Editions and de Appel, 2010, pp. 61–75.

Sikora, Matt and Kenneth Morris. *Gathering Visitor Feedback to Exhibition Design Before Designing the Exhibition*. Detroit: Michigan Museums Association Annual Conference, 2005.

Sikora, Matt, Daryl Fischer, Beverly Serrell, Deborah H. Perrt, and Ken Morris. "New Roles for Evaluation at the Detroit Institute of Arts." In "Focus on the Detroit Institute of Arts," Peter Linett (Ed.), special issue, *Curator: The Museum Journal* 52, 1 (January 2006): 45–65.

Simon, Nina. *The Participatory Museum*. Santa Cruz, CA: Museum 2.0, 2010.

Simon, Nina. "Participatory Design and the Future of Museums." In *Letting Go? Sharing Historical Authority in a User-Generated World*, edited by Bill Adair, Benjamin Filene, and Laura Koloski. Philadelphia: Pew Center for Arts and Heritage, 2011, pp. 18–33.

Silverman, Lois. "Visitor Meaning-Making in Museums for a New Age." *Curator: The Museum Journal* 38, 3 (September 1995): 161–170.

Silverman, Lois. *The Social Work of Museums*. Abingdon and New York: Routledge, 2010.

Smith, Terry. *Thinking Contemporary Curating*. New York: Independent Curators International, 2012.

Spalding, Julian. *The Eclipse of Art: Tackling the Crisis in Art Today*. Munich, London and New York: Prestel, 2003.

Spock, Daniel. "Is It Interactive Yet?" *Curator: The Museum Journal* 47, 4 (October 2004): 369–374.

Spock, Daniel. "The Puzzle of Museum Educational Practice: A Comment on Rounds and Falk." *Curator: The Museum Journal* 49, 2 (April 2006): 167–180.

Suchy, Sherene. "Emotional Intelligence, Passion and Museum Leadership." In *Reinventing the Museum: The Evolving Conversation on the Paradigm Shift*, edited by Gail Anderson. Lanham: AltaMira Press; 2nd Edition, 2012, pp. 451–467.

Tallant, Sally. "Experiments in Integrated Programming." In *Curating and the Educational Turn*, edited by Paul O'Neill and Mick Wilson. London and Amsterdam: Open Editions and de Appel, 2010, pp. 186–194.

Thea, Carolee and Thomas Micchelli (Eds.). *On Curating: Interviews with Ten International Curators*. New York: D.A.P., 2009.

Tilden, Freeman. *Interpreting Our Heritage*. 3rd Edition. Chapel Hill: University of North Carolina Press, 1957/1977.

Van den Bosch, Annette. "Museums: Constructing a Public Culture in the Global Age." In *Museums and Their Communities*, edited by Sheila Watson. London and New York: Routledge, 2007, pp. 501–509.

Vilk, Viktorya. *Display is Interpretation: Approaches to Integrating Interpretative Material in Six UK Galleries*. MA thesis. Leicester: University of Leicester, 2009.

Weil, Stephen. "The Museum and the Public." In *Museums and Their Communities*, edited by Sheila Watson. London and New York: Routledge, 2007, pp. 32–46.

Weil, Stephen E. "From Being *about* Something to being *for* Somebody: The Ongoing Transformation of the American Museum." In *Reinventing the Museum: The Evolving Conversation on the Paradigm Shift*, edited by Gail Anderson. Lanham: AltaMira Press; 2nd Edition, 2012, pp. 170–190.

Wells, Marcella, Barbara Butler, and Judith Koke. *Interpretive Planning for Museums: Integrating Visitor Perspectives in Decision Making*. Walnut Creek: Left Coast Press, Inc., 2013.

Wetterlund, Kris. *If You Can't See It, Don't Say It: A New Approach to Interpretive Writing*. Minneapolis: Museum-Ed, September 1, 2013. http://www.museum-ed.org/a-guide-to-interpretive-writing-about-art-for-museum-educators/

Wilk, Christopher and Nick Humphrey (Eds.). *Creating the British Galleries at the V&A: A Study in Museology*. London: V&A Publications and Goppion, 2004.

Williams, Patterson. "Object-Oriented Learning in Art Museums." *Roundtable Reports* 7, 2 (1982): 12–15.

Williams, Patterson. "Educational Excellence in Art Museums: An Agenda for Reform." *Journal of Aesthetic Education* 19, 2 (Summer 1985): 105–123.

Worts, Douglas. "Measuring Museum Meaning: A Critical Assessment Framework." *The Journal of Museum Education* 31, 1 (Spring 2006): 41–49.

Worts, Douglas. "Culture and Museums in the Winds of Change: The Need for Cultural Indicators." *Culture and Local Governance/Culture et gouvernance locale* 3, 1–2 (March 2011), pp. 117–132.

Zemer Ben-Ari, Hadas. "Live Encounter Tagging System/A Test Case Review." In *Workbook: An Art Mediation Resource*, edited by Yoeri Meessen and Thea Unteregger, pp. 1–6. Amsterdam, The Netherlands: Manifesta, nd. *Manifesta Workbook*. http://www.manifestaworkbook.org/Liveencounter.pdf

Index

access: to collections 130, 133, 137, 141; to curators 35, 40; to data 60, 175; interactive technology and electronic 175; for visitors 5, 34, 93, 149

activities: adult gallery activities 179; adventure playgrounds 67–9; collecting 51; creative activities 47, 56–7, 109–12, 117, 124, 134; daily 94; development of 105; evening activities 34–5, 99, 167; family-focused 5, 112; in-gallery activities 23, 25, 52, 56–7, 59, 61, 117–19, 123–4, 151–2; maker spaces 56–7; motivations 16; *You Are Here* 109–12

Adams, Marianna 102

Adjaye, David 156

admission-free museums 127, 129–42

advisors *see* consultants

advocacy 29, 36–7, 47, 49, 50–2, 54, 127, 129–30, 133, 137, 173

"An Agenda for Reform" (Williams) 51

ambiguity 173–4

art history: changing priorities for 114; contributing to discipline of 158; curatorial knowledge 39, 116; expertise 35–6; former curator moves beyond 20–2; motivations for studying 106; museum staff members trained in 115; reliance on information about 20; role of critical inquiry 145–6; staff members unschooled in 96–7; visitors without training in 15, 50, 120

Art Lab gallery (OMCA) 109–10

art museums: adult gallery activities at DIA 179; alienating their publics 21, 23; challenges of contemporary art for 9, 120–1, 146, 150–3, 159–60; challenges facing regional 115–17; different languages in 41; guidelines for thinking about and developing interpretation 14; history museums and 107–9; hybrid forms in 157; lack of reform efforts 18; lost context of 12–15, 35, 166; maintaining radicalism and relevance of artworks 146; misguided goal of reaching out to visitors 34–5; non-priorities of 113n4; prioritized for study 3, 177; reinvention practices at DIA 93; science museums and 108–9; as spaces of multiple/conflicting paths to truth/reality 150; as treasure house 91, 139, 145, 153; use of portable technology in 4; visitor-centered practice of DAM 49–54, 57, 60–1

art storage pods (Glasgow) 139

artifact 10, 58, 80, 85–6, 107

artworks: Denver Art Museum 49, 52, 57; Detroit Institute of Arts 97, 102–3; Van Abbe 146

assessment *see* evaluation

Association of Art Museum Curators (AAMC) 29, 38

audience *see* visitors

audience research: benefits of 38, 166; CMA 114; de-emphasis on 63; DIA 103; DMA 47, 54; focus groups 14–16; Kelvingrove Gallery 24, 127, 131–3; label-writing power struggle based on 31; limitations 3; method 178; MNHS 86, 169; OMCA 105, 169; traditional collection-based museums 91

audio tours 17, 151

authority 29, 39, 93, 159

Baie, Sarah 156, 158
barriers 5, 21, 32, 36, 42, 133
Bead Studio, The (DAM) 59
Beal, Graham 20–2, 26, 93, 96–7, 103
Bellamy, Martin 131–2, 134
benches *see* seating
Berndes, Christiane 36, 153
Big-E evaluations 54, 60, 102, 170
Big Ideas 97–8, 104n1, 170
Blomberg, Nancy 57, 58–9, 60
board members 1, 67, 69, 91, 156, 158
Borsdorf, Ulrich 72–4, 75, 80
Botticelli, Sandro 129
Bourdieu, Pierre 33–4, 132
briefing books 73–4

case studies: City Museum, St. Louis 3, 65–9; Columbus Museum of Art 3, 114–26; continuum of approaches to connecting with visitors 46, 165–7; data 178; Denver Art Museum 3, 49–61; Detroit Institute of Arts 3, 93–104; interview protocol 178; Kelvingrove Gallery 3, 129–42; method 177–8; Minnesota History Center 3, 82–90; Oakland Museum of California 3, 105–13; Ruhr Museum, Essen, Germany 3, 70–81; Van Abbe Museum, Eindhoven, NL 3, 145–54
Cassilly, Bob 67–9, 72, 155, 166
Cassilly, Gail 67
Chambers, Marlene 35, 47, 50
change: benefits of 36–8; challenges of 27, 30–2, 41–2, 45, 93, 105, 110, 115–16, 120–1, 169, 171–2; Change Cycle 33; closing gap in understanding 36–9; contours of 27–42; dumbing down 29–30; gap in understanding 34–5; loss and 32–4; new models 39–42; new power dynamics 28–9; reframing 38–42; structural change 6–7; turf wars 30–1; types of 4–7; visitor-centered approach in exhibitions 4–5; war stories 31–2; *see also* organizational change
children 14, 22–3, 57, 67, 68, 74, 101, 127, 134–5
children's museums 23, 82, 84
City Museum, St. Louis: in case studies continuum 166; case study 3, 65–9; collections 67; as founder-driven

museum 63, 68, 72; Maker Culture 67; management team 68–9; pilgrimage environments 67
Clark, T.J. 146
Cloud Gate (Kapoor) 13
cognitive overload/disconnect 81, 158
collaboration: with community 122, 142; with contemporary artists 120; with curators 29, 38, 41, 97, 147, 156; with exhibition designers 54; information and 60–1; of Lerner and Baie 156; staff collaboration 4, 145, 153, 172; team approach 17; teams 6, 22, 27–9, 36–7, 41–2, 83, 90, 108–9, 141; teamwork 122; trust-building exercises/workshops 42; visitors 117
collection-based museums: Columbus Museum of Art 91, 114–25; Denver Art Museum 49–61; Detroit Institute of Arts 91, 93–103; Kelvingrove Museum and Gallery 129–42; Oakland Museum of California 91, 105–12; Ruhr Museum 70–81; Van Abbe Museum 145–54
Columbus Museum of Art: in case studies continuum 166; case study 3, 114–26; "The Changing Landscape" gallery 114; commitment to visitors 114; "connectors" 114, 117–18, 125; evaluation 120; "Join the Conversation" Post-it bulletin boards 118; mission statement 116; museum protocol 122–3; voting stations 119
comfort 5, 10
communication 6, 11, 14, 42
community advisory panels 106; *see also* visitor panels
competition 73, 132
"connectors" (CMA) 114, 117–18, 125
connoisseurs *see* experts
consultants 98, 102, 104, 109, 116, 169–71
contemporary art 9, 17–18, 120, 125, 145, 149, 153, 158, 160
contemporary artists 120–1, 145, 149, 153
content design 20, 22, 73
content specialists 17, 74, 83, 173
context *see* museum context
control: "controlled chaos" 84; of display space for contemporary

artists 120; evoking trauma of WWII and 87; in science museums 35; lack of 69; loss of curatorial 28–31, 42; visitor choice and control 6
controversy 24, 97, 127, 135–6
conversation 25, 28, 30, 36–7, 40, 59, 96, 105, 108, 114, 151, 165, 170, 176; with CMA museum staff 120; with community and behind the scenes 89; conversation boards 118, 123; with gallery attendants 17; with game masters 152; in outcome of CMA's shared vocabulary 117; of objects and stories 82–4; "structured conversations" with visitors 54
cooperation *see* collaboration
Cortez, Jaime 105
counter-narrative 149
creative activities *see* activities
critical inquiry 145–6
critical/meta-thinking 117, 153, 167
critical reflection 145–6, 150, 152–3, 167
critics 13, 24, 29–31, 33, 54, 132–3, 160, 176
Crown Fountain (Plensa) 13
Csikszentmihalyi, Mihalyi 16
cultural value 94, 176
"Curatorial Practice and the Educational Turn" 38
curators: accusations of dumbing down 29–30, 116; benefits of change 36–8; challenges facing 169; closing gap in understanding 36; collaboration 29, 38, 41, 60–1, 90, 97; collaboration with educators 147; conversations with people 120; gallery installation 121; gap in understanding 34–5; hybrid position 40–1; in "Kellogg Model" 173; installing history exhibitions 108; lack of 156; new power dynamics for 28–9; reactions and concerns to change 29–34; as resource people 97; role in label writing 97–8; structural change for 6; teams and 27–8; traditional model 20–1, 49; training up 174–5; turf wars 30–1; working with evaluators 170
curiosity: children and 67–8, 84; curiosity-driven visitor 168; in outcome of CMA's shared vocabulary 117; as motivator 141; pent-up

public curiosity 72; receptivity and 111; sparking 70; value of just-in-time information for 102
Czajkowski, Jennifer 101

data 38, 51, 60, 61, 178
DenkSchrift 73
Dent, Lisa 120–1
Denver Art Museum: adult gallery activities at 179; American Indian collection 57–9, 60; The Bead Studio 59; in case studies continuum 166; case study 3, 49–61; "Discovery Library" 52; "Fashion Studio" 60; Hamilton Building 49, 54, 57; *installed interpretives* 52; Interpretation Project 52; interpretive support for art 35; maker spaces 56–7; "Marvelous Mud" 59; "Mud Studio" 59; multi-year action research project 52; seating 47, 50, 52, 54, 56, 61; Thread Studio 59; use of evaluators 170; wall text/labels 60
designers: challenges facing 169; collaboration with curators and subject-focused educators 56, 59–60; in core teams 83, 90; exhibition designers 47, 49, 54–6; experience designers/developers 27, 39–40, 42, 110, 112, 120, 145, 147; gallery installation 121; in dialogue about audience 2; in "Kellogg Model" 173; installing history exhibitions 108; role of audience research for 169; structural change for 6, 22; working with outside groups 138
destination experience: destination museum 20, 29, 137; non-destination cities 45, 91, 105, 112, 114–16, 125, 176n4; permanent exhibitions 83, 90
Detroit Institute of Arts: case study 3, 93–104; community response 103; evaluation 102–3; Graham Beal 96; museum mission 20–2; new forms of gallery interpretation 100–2; pull-out panels 100–1; reinstallation of galleries 96; *Splendor by the Hour* 95–6, 102; visitor-centered interpretation techniques 96–9; visitor experience 93–6; visitor panels 180
dialogue: about audience 2; among museum professionals 15; between community partners and collection

curators 138; with contemporary
artists 145; with Game Master 152;
between high and low culture 157,
161; improving 42; insider-outsider
dialogue 25; internal collaboration
and 122; open dialogue 172–3;
prompting 176; role of 147; with
viewers 150
Dierking, Lynn D. 168
directors *see* museum directors
"Discovery Library" (DAM) 52
docents: docent tours 84, 141; docent
training 21–2; visitor comfort and
10, 167; *see also* gallery assistants/
attendants/guides/hosts
double empathy 14, 121, 169
dumbing down 29–30, 116, 133,
167, 176

education: AAMC panel on educational
turn 38; alternative 156–7, 160;
education curators 41; education
department 40; experience designer/
developer role 145, 153; funding 28;
gallery-based education 52; identity
and 33; importance of 24; integration
with curatorial vision 174; issues
of museum education 17; learning
culture 172–3; prioritized at DAM
54; prioritized in city of Glasgow
127, 132–3; role in creating visitor-
centered ideas 22; shortcomings
of formal education system 88;
traditional roles 50
educators: challenges facing 169;
collaboration with curators 37, 56,
59–60, 147; collaboration with
designers 56, 59–60; conversations
with people 120; in core teams 83,
90; installing history exhibitions 108;
lack of 156; new power dynamics
for 27–30; in organizational
hierarchies 51; role in label writing
97–8; structural change for 6, 22;
traditional model 49; traditional
roles 159; training 174; work with
exhibition development 173; working
with evaluators 170
Eliasson, Olafur 13
El Lissitzky 147, 149
emotional connection: with artwork
at CMA 114, 119; context for 35;
curatorial challenges for providing
41, 166; goal of reaching out to
visitors and creating 64; "human
connection cards" 52; with objects
and stories at Ruhr 70, 75; with
objects at Canadian Museum of
Civilization 11; as part of mission
of MNHS 83–4; play and 69; staff
training up for 174
empathy 14, 99, 103, 121
engagement: DAM focus on fostering
visitor creative engagement
59; Engagement curator 38;
Engagement Officer 114, 121–2,
125; experimental approach to
visitor engagement 143; with gallery
attendants in conversations 17;
Kelvingrove program of 133; mission
of MNHS 63–4; of novices and
amateurs with artworks 52; physical
engagement 69; prototyping projects
and 109, 112, 112n4; through
audience immersion 90, 166; visitor-
centered approach for 4–5; visitor
panels 98; works and environments
for broad public 13
Erwin, Rick, III 67–8
Esche, Charles 143, 145–6, 152
evaluation: ad hoc informal evaluation
120; based on goals of visitor 168;
Big-E (summative) 54, 60, 102, 170;
economical evaluation techniques
50–1; experimentation and 52–4,
60; lack of 69; OMCA team-based
approach 108; prototyping projects
and 112n4; reevaluation 2; reports
110; small-e (formative or informal)
54, 109–10, 120, 170; surveys 50,
106; target audience 132–3; tracking
and timing 102–3, 170, 176n1;
see also audience research
evaluators 22, 99, 102, 112, 116,
170, 173
Evans, Catherine 116
exhibitions: exhibition architects 74;
exhibition catalogues 35; exhibition
design 22, 47, 51; exhibition
designers 73; exhibition development
4–5, 47, 83, 108; exhibition
programs 23; pre-packaged traveling
exhibitions 159
experience designers/developers
27, 39–40, 42, 110, 112, 120,
145, 147

experimentation: audience research and 103; at CMA 114, 117, 125; collaboration with visitors 117; with collection-free ways of engaging audiences 23; creating thriving learning culture through 172; at DIA 99; at DMA 57; evaluation and 52–4, 60; freedom for 45; at MCA Denver 143, 155; necessity of 122; at OMCA 110; reinvigorating traditional museums through 91; use of technology in 17–18; at Van Abbe Museum 143, 146, 151, 153

expertise: audience expertise 20–1, 39, 47, 51, 98; collection expertise 54; consultants 170; curatorial expertise 153; deference of visitors to 9; dumbing down and 167; earning of 35; in-house expertise 143; insider-outsider dialogue incorporation 25; lack of 114; levels of 180; local artists demonstrating 59; museum expertise 169; of museum professionals 2; realms in new teams 28; reframing 38–9, 175; subject expertise 5; traditional museum roles 20–2

experts: in audiences 51; content experts 83; dumbing down and 167; expert viewers 127; gap in understanding between general public and 34; information in galleries and 36; levels of expertise 180; magic experts 16; museum policy for access to objects 141; outside experts 102; role in label writing 97–8; subject matter experts 90; traditional museum roles 20–2

Falk, John 16, 168
families 5, 16, 25, 84, 88, 125, 133–4
family programs 157–8
"Fashion Studio" (DAM) 60
findings *see* data
Fischer, Daryl 98–9
flow experiences 6, 73
focus groups 14–16, 21, 50, 69, 98
Fogarty, Lori 22–3, 38, 105, 106, 107, 108, 170, 173
Foley, Cindy 116
foraging theory 168
friends 5, 13, 16, 84, 88
front end research *see* evaluation
fundraisers 157–8

galleries: contemporary art installations in 121; as context-rich environments 54–6; gallery-based interpretation programs 161; reinstallation 56, 96, 108, 133–7; white cube gallery space 12, 17
gallery assistants/attendants/guides/ hosts 17–18, 23, 101, 121, 126n1, 151, 167; *see also* docents
gallery interpretation: City 68–9; CMA 114–15, 117–19, 125; DAM 49, 51–60; DIA 93–6, 100–2; as element common to visitor-centered museums 45; in traditional museums 91; Kelvingrove 130–1, 134–7; MCA Denver 158–61, 166–8; MNHS 83–7; OMCA 107–8, 109–12; Ruhr 74–81; Van Abbe 143, 147–53; *see also* interpretation
"Game Masters" (VAB) 151–2, 167
games 25, 52, 54, 117, 134, 143, 151–2, 166
Gehry, Frank 13
Glasgow Life 132
goals: to assist visitors to have peak experiences 41, 51–2, 114, 119; of audience-centric vision 25; collaboration 42, 171; to create emotional connections 64; of curiosity-driven visitor 168; label writing 151; learning 68, 88; of museum visits 16; of reaching out to visitors 34; of reinstallation 133
Grainland (MNHS) 83
Gretzky, Wayne 11
Gurian, Elaine Heumann 129
Gutnik, Earl 83
Guzman, René de 40–1, 108, 174

Hamilton Building 49, 54, 57
Hart, Becky 97
Heimlich, Joe 116
Heinrich, Christoph 54
Heinzen, Jesse 87
Henry, Barbara 106
high culture 33, 132, 157, 161
history museums 35, 73, 74, 82, 106–8, 109, 127, 129
Höller, Carsten 13
Home Place, Minnesota (MNHS) 87
"human connection cards" 49, 54, 57

ideas 97–8, 104n1, 170
identity: institutional 9–10, 22–3, 46, 103, 114, 117, 127, 132, 155–6, 158; social class 33; visitor 99, 160–1
Impressionists 129–30
in-gallery interactive activities: Columbus Museum of Art 117–25; Denver Art Museum 52; Detroit Institute of Arts 93–103; Kelvingrove Gallery 130–42; Oakland Museum of California 23, 106–13
Insights: Museums, Visitors, Attitudes, Expectations: A Focus Group Experiment (J. Paul Getty Trust) 14
interactive art games 114, 118, 134, 151–2
interdisciplinarity 15, 109
interpretation: "connectors" 114, 117–18, 125; conversations and 151; curator 35; dumbing down of interpretive content 133; in-gallery activities 25, 45, 50–2, 54–6; installed interpretives 52, 60, 61, 114, 135–67; interpretive communication 14; interpretive deficit 21; issues of 157, 160, 161; meaningfulness of 132; provocation and 14, 18n1, 167–8; role of history 59; role of information in 14, 35–6; techniques 96–102; *see also* gallery interpretation
interpretive specialists 3, 20, 27, 37, 93
interviews: about prototyping 108; with contemporary Indian artists 58–9; interview protocol 178; for study 2–3, 7, 28; visitor interviews 16, 50, 51–2, 54
iteration 52–4, 60

Johnson, Annie 84, 86
just-in-time 17, 54, 102, 166, 170

Kapoor, Anish 13
Kelvingrove Gallery, Glasgow, UK: in case studies continuum 166–7; case study 3, 129–42; collection storage facility 139; *Conflict and Consequence* 130–1; criticism 132ff; Glasgow Life 132; mandate for public access 141; museum mission 23–5; Nitshill Open Storage 127, 139, 142; Open Museum 137–9; reinstallation 129, 133–7; renovation

129–30; school groups 141; social mission 127, 132; target audience 132–3; thematizing of collections 133–4; using startling juxtapositions to provoke new insights 130–1
Koolhaas, Rem 71
Koons, Jeff 12
Krupp, Alfred 79

La Riccia, Tracey 68
Lab, The 156
label writing: role of consultants in 170; role of curators in 20; role of educators in 97–8; structural change for 22; team dialogue in 173; turf wars 30–1
labels *see* label writing; wall text/labels
language: barriers 21, 32, 41–2; hermetic language 10, 105; museum language 10, 33; wall text/labels 21, 23, 54, 166, 170
layered labels 101–2
leadership: growing into and staying the course 171–2; initiating change 20–6; leading organizational change 169; reconsideration of key museum roles by 6–7; *see also* museum directors
lecture series 156–7
Lerner, Adam 143, 155, 156, 157, 159, 160
lessons: in art history 21; from a learning team 82–90; museum manners 57
Libeskind, Daniel 49, 54
Live Encounter Tagging System (LETS) 150–1
live events 159, 160, 167
Long, Richard 114
"low" culture 157, 161

Maciejunes, Nannette 114, 174
maker spaces 51, 56–7
Marcil, Pam 97
"Marvelous Mud" (DAM) 59
Matisse, Henri-Émile-Benoît 146
McDermott-Lewis, Melora 49, 52, 60
McLean, Kathleen 109, 173
meaning-making strategies 102–3
media presentations 86–7
Mercer, Valerie 97
Merz, Hans Günter 73–4, 75
metaphors for museums: as asymmetrical bridges 16; as a brand

155; community living room 114–25;
as cultural commons 129–42; as
a new kind of townsquare 167; as
a resource 159; as toolset 145; as
treasure house 91, 145, 153
Metropolitan Museum of Art 54, 116
Minnesota History Center (MNHS):
in case studies continuum 166;
case study 3, 82–90; collections
82, 84–5; core audience 85; core
team 83; exhibition prototyping
88–9; exhibitions on view at 83–7;
generative process of 83; goal of
88–90; *Grainland* 83; *Home Place,
Minnesota* 87; informed by spirit of
play 167; media presentations 86–7;
Minnesota's Greatest Generation
83, 84, 85–7; museum mission 63;
Open House 83, 85; relations with
Dakota Indians 88–9; teams 83; use
of audience research 169; *Weather
Permitting* 83, 84
Minnesota's Greatest Generation
(MNHS) 83, 84, 85–7
mistakes, freedom to make 153, 172
Mixed Taste (MCA) 156–7, 160
Monet, Claude 119
Mostov, Merilee 114, 117–18, 120, 122
"Mud Studio" (DAM) 59
multimedia interactives 17, 58–9
Museum of Contemporary Art,
Denver: Adam Lerner/Sarah Baie
156; audience 158; in case studies
continuum 167; case study 3,
155–61; as creative workshop
143; galleries 158; gallery-based
interpretation programs 161;
improvisational exploration 155–6;
lecture series 156–7; live events
159; *Mixed Taste* 156–7, 160;
next-generation institution 155;
organizational chart 156; primary
emphasis of 158–9; *Unauthenticated
Paintings of the Russian Avant-Garde*
158–9; weakness of 159–60
museum context: adult gallery
activities at DMA 179; appropriate
environment for enhancing
experience 87; in case studies
continuum 166; for connecting
people to stories 116; cultural and
historical context of objects 18,
39; different languages of curators

and educators in 41; for history
museums 107, 166; "interpretive
deficit" and 21; as intimidating
9–10; lack of context 12; lost
context of art museums 12–15, 35,
166; for maintaining radicalism
and relevance of artworks 116,
146; offering interpretive paths and
activities for non-specialist viewers
54–6; preferential access for trustees
and collectors 35; as spaces of
multiple/conflicting paths to truth/
reality 150; staff training 175; use
of interpretive tools in 101–2; use of
technology to restore context 17
museum directors: Adam Lerner 143,
155, 156, 157, 159, 160; building
cross-disciplinary teams 41–2;
challenges 41–2, 115–16; Charles
Esche 143, 145–6, 152; Christoph
Heinrich 54; Dan Spock 82, 85, 87,
158, 172–3, 174; Graham Beal 20–2,
26, 93, 96–7, 103; growing into and
staying the course 171–2; growing
into leadership and staying the course
171–2; on inevitability of change
in museums 1–2; initiating change
20–6; leading organizational change
169; Lewis Sharp 54; Lori Fogarty
22–3, 105, 106, 107, 170, 173; Mark
O'Neill 23–5, 127, 129–30, 133,
137; Melora McDermott-Lewis 49,
52, 60; Nannette Maciejunes 114,
174; reconsideration of key museum
roles by 6–7; Rick Erwin III 67–8;
Ulrich Borsdorf 72–4, 75, 80
museum mission: creating new teams
27–8; of finding personal meaning
in artworks 99; fundamental
reconsideration of 1–4; impact of
data on 38; of reveling in play spirit
158; role of children inspiring 22–3
museum mission statements 23, 69, 116
museum voice 30, 76, 93, 100, 117
museums: creating learning culture
172–3; as cultural commons 129–42;
double empathy 14, 169; engaging
through audience immersion 63–90;
founder-driven museums 63;
historical collections 47, 49–61; as
immersive sites 63–90; interpretive
practices 167–8; as intimidating
spaces 9–10; living with ambiguity

173–4; moving forward 174–5; "museum as treasure house" model of presentation 153; museum culture 39; museum manners 57; museum protocol 122–3; provocation 167–8; security personnel 17; social mission 4, 158; social museum mission 23; studied 2–3; taking the long view 175–6; traditional approach 20–2; traditional collection-based museums 93–126; training 174–5; visitor-centered continuum 165–7; wall color 117, 125; *see also* gallery interpretation; interpretation; metaphors for museums

narratives 84, 133, 149–50, 154
new positions 39–40
Nielsen, Heather 57, 59
Nitshill Open Storage 127, 139, 142
non-visitors 9, 15, 98, 133, 191

Oakland Museum of California (OMCA): attending to the public 38; case study 3, 105–13; diverse communities of 105–6; gallery redesign 106; history galleries 108; as interdisciplinary museum, 107; OMCA Lab 106; Owner's Manual 170; Philosophy of Interpretation 106–7; reinstallation 108; team-based approach 108–9; use of audience research 169; use of evaluators 170; vision 22; *You Are Here* 109–12
"Object-Oriented Learning in Art Museums" (Williams) 51
objects: appreciation of 15; curatorial knowledge of 32; gap in understanding 34–5; in intimidating museum 9; memory trigger 70–1, 73, 75, 76, 86, 102, 129, 138; museum policy for access to 141; offering interpretive hooks for 10–11; presentation and role at MNHS 83–90; presentation at CMA 118–25, 166; presentation at DAM 51, 58–9, 166; presentation at DIA 94–6, 100–3; presentation at Kelvingrove 130–41, 166–7; presentation at MNHS 166; presentation at OMCA 23–5, 109–12; presentation at Ruhr 70, 72–4, 75–81, 166; presentation at

Van Abbe 145–51; technology and 17–18; in traditional museums 21; at Van Abbe Museum 167
O'Neill, Mark 23–5, 127, 129–30, 133, 137
Open Conversations: Strategies for Professional Development in Museums (Blackmon, LaMaster, Roberts & Serrell) 16, 83
Open House (MNHS) 83, 85
Open Museum 137–9
open storage 127, 139
organization: hierarchies 6, 27, 42, 51, 99, 169; structural change for 6–7; transformation of 4, 7, 23, 153, 156
organizational change: at CMA 122; at DAM 47, 49–54, 60–1; at DIA 22, 93, 97, 98; at Kelvingrove 24–7, 138–43; leading 169, 171–2; at MCA Denver 155, 158; new power dynamics for 28; at OMCA 23, 25, 27, 105; for promoting visitor-centered approach in exhibitions 4–5, 45; teams working across disciplines 41–2; at Van Abbe 145, 153; *see also* change
outcomes 31, 98, 116–18, 169, 174; *see also* evaluation
outreach 137, 138
outsider intimidation 96–7

Paterson, Laurel 98
Paying Attention: Visitors and Museum Exhibitions (Serrell) 168
Payton, Cydney 156
peak experiences 41, 51–2, 114, 119
"People" wall (OMCA) 110–11
Picasso, Pablo 146
play: at City Museum 63, 65–9, 166; at CMA 115, 117, 123; at MCA Denver 155, 158, 160–1; at MNHS 63–4, 82, 84, 88, 166; at Van Abbe 145, 149, 151–3, 167
Play Van Abbe: overview of 151–3; personas 151–2, 154n4; purpose of 145
Plensa, Jaume 13
Pollock, Jackson 146
Ponti, Gio 49, 52
power 28–31, 42
principles, guiding *see* museum mission
professional training, recommendations for 174–5
project managers 27, 83, 90

props 169–71
prototyping: exhibition prototyping at MNHS 88–9, 112, 112n4, 169; exhibition prototyping at OMCA 108–10, 112, 112n4, 169; use of small-e evaluation for 54; visitor panels at DIA 100
provocation 14, 167–8
Pubols, Louise 108
Puppy (Koons) 12
purpose *see* museum mission

Quenroe, Elroy 57

radical hospitality 143, 145, 153, 168
Rand, Judy 5–6, 38, 107
reframing: connecting through adaptive reuse and design 70–4; "curator-educator hybrid, curator-marketer" 40–1; display of artworks 49–60, 93–5, 117–25, 147–51; experience designer 39–40; history 82–9; interdisciplinarity and 109; Lori Fogarty on 38–9; museum experience 65–9; new models for 39–42; offering interpretive hooks for 10–11; open storage 137–41; teams working across disciplines 41–2; using juxtapositions to provoke new insights 130–1
reinstallation 56, 96, 108, 133–7
Rembrandt Van Rijn 129
Rinaldi, Ray Mark 160
Roberts, Kate 82, 83
roles: changing roles for community 138; changing roles for curators 97–8; changing roles for museum directors 171; changing roles for museum practice 143, 145, 153, 155, 158, 167; changing roles for museum professionals 6–7, 93; role play 151; therapeutic role of museum 132–3
Ruhr Museum, Essen, Germany: case study 3, 70–81; collections 71, 75–81; data visualization zone 74; development of 73–4; entrance 71; as founder-driven museum 63; in case studies continuum 166; parade of native species 79; scenographies 79; site of 70; visitor experience 74–81
Rummel, Rich 84, 85, 87

Sayre, Scott 35
school groups 50, 68, 139, 141

science museums 35, 108
seating: Columbus Museum of Art 116, 118, 120; comfort and 5; debate over 34; Denver Art Museum 47, 50, 52, 54, 56, 61; Oakland Museum of California 23, 111
Serrell, Beverly 102, 168
Sharp, Lewis 54
signage *see* wall text/labels
Sikora, Matt 99, 169
Simon, Nina 158
Sly, Jennifer 83
small-e evaluations 54, 109–10, 120, 170
Smith, Terry 35, 38
Solakov, Nedko 149
Sorgenicht, Sandra 74
Spirit of St. Louis 10
Splendor by the Hour 95–6, 102
Spock, Dan: on creating learning culture 172–3; on formal education system 88; on hooks 85; on living with ambiguity 174; on museum-going as form of play 88, 158, 167; priorities for 82; reflections on *Minnesota's Greatest Generation* and its evocation of war 87
staff members 15, 22, 42, 96, 99, 155, 172
stories: challenges facing regional museums connecting people to 116; at DIA 93–7, 101; at Kelvingrove 130, 133, 139; at MNHS 63, 82–9; at OMCA 107; role at Kelvingrove 130; at Ruhr 70, 75–81; war stories 31–2
structural change 6–7
Sudler, James 49

Tate Modern 13
teams *see* collaboration
technology: AAMC panel on 38; courses 174, 175; interdisciplinarity and 109; lack of 69; limitations of 17–18; *Play Van Abbe* 152; rare instance of 74; specialist 83; technology-based interpretation 167; use of digital technology in museums 3–4; use at Kelvingrove 138–9; use of participatory 112
therapeutic role of museum 132–3
Thread Studio (DAM) 59
Tilden, Freeman 14, 18n1, 167

tracking and timing studies 102, 170, 176n1
trustees 9–10, 16, 32, 36, 137
turf wars 30–1; *see also* organizational change

Unauthenticated Paintings of the Russian Avant-Garde (MCA) 158–9
U.S. National Parks Service 14
user-generated content *see* visitor participation

Van Abbe Museum, Eindhoven, NL: case study 3, 145–54; collaboration 153; creating learning culture 172–3; as creative workshop 143; critical reflection 145; El Lissitzky exhibition 147–9; experience designers 39–40; experimentation 146; "Game Masters" 151; in case studies continuum 167; Live Encounter Tagging System 150–1; *Play Van Abbe* 145, 151–3, 154n4; *radical hospitality* 143, 145
Van Drasek, Stephanie 67–8
videos 58–9
visitor-centered continuum 46, 165–7
visitor-centered interpretation techniques *see* interpretation
visitor-centered mission 3, 23, 45, 47, 51, 61, 121, 125, 127
visitor experience: City Museum 65–9; Columbus Museum of Art 114–25; Denver Art Museum 52–60; Detroit Institute of Arts 93–103; just-in-time 17, 54, 102, 166, 170; Kelvingrove Gallery 130–41; Minnesota History Center 83–90; Museum of Contemporary Art 157–61; Oakland Museum of California 109–12; Ruhr Museum 71–81; Van Abbe Museum 147–53; visitor-centered approach 4–5
visitor feedback/input 4, 50, 54, 60, 93, 97, 99, 106, 110, 121–2, 169–70; *see also* audience research; focus groups; visitor panels
visitor panels 60, 69, 98–9, 100, 180
visitor participation: benefits of 37–8; City Museum 65–9; Columbus

Museum of Art 117–20, 122–5; Denver Art Museum 52, 56–60; Detroit Institute of Arts 98–102; Kelvingrove 25; Kelvingrove Gallery 133–41; Minnesota History Center 86–90, 166, 174; Museum of Contemporary Art 157, 160; Oakland Museum of California 110–12; Ruhr Museum 74–83; Van Abbe Museum 143, 146, 149–53
visitor questions 6, 17, 18, 22, 88, 94, 99, 105, 106, 157
visitors: "advanced amateurs" 52; "art novices" 52; behavior patterns 51–2; considering 9–18; curiosity–driven visitor 168; "diligent visitors" 168; expert viewers 127; feedback 54, 60, 120–1, 169, 170; goal of reaching out to 34–5; interpretive paths and activities for non-specialist viewers 54–6; motivations 16; prioritizing 27, 31, 39, 41, 45, 51, 90, 127, 134, 165, 168; return visitors 26, 45, 67, 91, 114–15, 129; tracking and timing studies 102; values 99
Visitors' Bill of Rights 5–6, 38, 107
Visual Thinking Strategies 17–18
Visual Velcro 4, 10, 13, 15, 84, 102, 117–18, 121, 166; *see also* emotional connection
voices: curatorial voice 25; insider/ outsider voices 25; museum voice 30, 76, 93, 100, 117
volunteers 6, 22, 141, 151

wall text/labels: CMA 117, 125; DAM 54, 60; DIA 93–8, 100–2; Kelvingrove 134; label writing 20, 22, 30–1, 97–8, 170, 173; layered labels 101–2; tailored to audience interests 5; Van Abbe 150–1
Weather Permitting (MNHS) 83, 84
Weather Project, The (Eliasson) 13
white cube gallery space 12, 17
Williams, Patterson 47, 49–52, 54

You Are Here (OMCA) 109–12

Zemer Ben-Ari, Hadas 39–40, 146–7, 151